THE MADE-UP SELF

THE MADE-UP

Self

*Impersonation in
the Personal Essay*

CARL H. KLAUS

University of Iowa Press

Iowa City

University of Iowa Press,
Iowa City 52242
Copyright © 2010 by Carl H. Klaus
www.uiowapress.org
Printed in the United States of America
Design by Richard Hendel

Early versions of essays in this book
have been published as follows:
"Montaigne on His Essays: Toward a
Poetics of Self," *Iowa Review* (Winter
1991): 1–23; "Excursions of the Mind:
Toward a Poetics of Uncertainty in the
Disjunctive Essay," *What Do I Know:
Reading, Writing, and Teaching the Essay*,
edited by Janis Forman (Heinemann,
1994), pp. 39–53; "The Chameleon
'I': On Voice and Personality in the
Personal Essay," *Voices on Voice*, edited
by Kathleen Blake Yancey (National
Council of Teachers of English, 1995),
pp. 111–29; and "Embodying the Self:
Malady and the Personal Essay," *Iowa
Review* (Spring/Summer 1995): 177–92.

The University of Iowa Press is a
member of Green Press Initiative and
is committed to preserving natural
resources.

Printed on acid-free paper

Library of Congress
Cataloging-in-Publication Data
Klaus, Carl H.
The made-up self: impersonation in
the personal essay / by Carl H. Klaus.
p.   cm.
Includes bibliographical references
and index.
ISBN-13: 978-1-58729-913-1 (pbk.)
ISBN-10: 1-58729-913-5 (pbk.)
ISBN-13: 978-1-58729-946-9 (ebook)
ISBN-10: 1-58729-946-1 (ebook)
1. Essays—Authorship.   I. Title.
PN4500.K59 2010
808.4—dc22   2010007650

To the persons

who urged it into being,

JACQUELINE BLANK

KATE FRANKS KLAUS

ROBERT SCHOLES

Painting myself for others, I have
painted my inward self with colors
clearer than my original ones.
—Michel de Montaigne, "Of Giving the Lie"

That specific "I" is, of course, a construction.
I continually make her up as I go along out
of whatever materials come to hand.
—Nancy Mairs, "Prelude"

CONTENTS

The sense of a human presence that animates a personal essay is surely one of the most beguiling literary phenomena, for it usually comes across in so familiar and direct a voice, seemingly without effort or contrivance, that it's easy to believe I'm hearing (or overhearing) the author of the piece rather than a textual stand-in. Listen to Montaigne tell about his near-fatal fall from a horse, or Virginia Woolf about the death of a moth, or James Baldwin about his sojourn in a Swiss mountaintop village, or Joan Didion about keeping a notebook, or Vivian Gornick about street-life in New York City, and you will hear such distinctive voices that you too might refer to the persons in those pieces by the names of the authors who created them, as if they were one and the same. And in a sense they are, given the self-referential status of "I" that's entrenched in language. A personal essay does, after all, put one more directly in contact with the thought and feeling of its author than do other forms of literature, if only because personal essayists speak in their own name rather than through the fictive characters that inhabit the work of novelists and playwrights.

But the "person" in a personal essay is a written construct, a fabricated thing, a character of sorts — the sound of its voice a by-product of carefully chosen words, its recollection of experience, its run of thought and feeling, much tidier than the mess of memories, thoughts, and feelings arising in one's consciousness. As Scott Russell Sanders says in "The Singular First Person," "What we meet on the page is not the flesh and blood author, but a simulacrum, a character who wears the label I." Indeed, when personal essayists write about self-embodiment in the essay, they often acknowledge an element of fabrication or of artful impersonation. Montaigne admits in "Of Giving the Lie" that "Painting my self for others, I have painted my inward self with colors clearer than the original ones." Charles Lamb in an unpublished review praises William Haz-

1

litt for the "assumption of a character . . . which gives force and life to his writing." In "The Modern Essay," Virginia Woolf dramatizes the paradox of essayistic self-embodiment in a striking imperative: "Never to be yourself and yet always—that is the problem." Likewise, Vivian Gornick tells of discovering the need for a persona "who was me and at the same time was not me." Edward Hoagland doesn't even nod at the possibility of being oneself, suggesting in "What I Think, What I Am" that "the artful 'I' of an essay can be as chameleon as any narrator in fiction." E. B. White in a letter about his work (August 15, 1969), frankly acknowledges that "Writing is a form of imposture: I'm not at all sure I am anything like the person I seem to a reader." And Nancy Mairs, whose self-revelatory essays in *Carnal Acts* might seem to be unrehearsed confessions, declares in "But First," that "I am not the woman whose voice animates my essays. She's made up."

The "made-up" self and the manifold ways it has come to life in a wide range of essayists and essays—these are my central concerns in this book. Thus it is intended to reconceive the most fundamental element of the personal essay—the "I" of the essayist—and by doing so to demonstrate that this seemingly uncontrived form of writing is inherently problematic. I don't mean to suggest that it's devious or willfully misleading like some fictionalized memoirs of recent years. But it's well to remember that the world of literary nonfiction borders upon the world of fiction, and sometimes their boundaries overlap, as Phillip Lopate implies in his Foreword to *The Essays of Elia*: "all autobiographical first persons are highly selective and therefore distorting representations of their owners, even when they do not bother, as Lamb did, to employ an alter ego or pen name." Lopate's observation is a reminder too that whenever we write in the first person, reflecting on our personal experience, we inevitably create a version of ourselves, crafting a self out of words.

Though the essayist's "I" has not been the subject of a book-length study, personal essayists have shed light on it in so many different contexts—in prefaces, introductions, essays, reviews, diaries, letters, and interviews—that I have collected and analyzed their comments and been guided by them in the conception and organization of this book, as well as in my approach to specific authors, issues, and texts. In defining or describing a persona, essayists tend to emphasize either consciousness or personality—either interiority or exteriority. Thus I have devoted the first two parts of this book to "Evocations of Consciousness" and "Evocations of Personality," each of which focuses on representative authors and texts as a means of exploring how structure, style, and voice determine the nature of a persona and one's perception of it. My reading and writing of essays have also led me to realize that a persona is inevitably shaped by both the impress of culture and the force of personal experience. Accordingly, the last two parts of this book are devoted to "Personae and Culture" and "Personae and Personal Experience," as reflected in the point of view, content, and voice of selected essays and essayists.

Given my addiction to the personal essay, I could not resist the temptation to write about it in the freewheeling form of essays, nor could I resist the enticing roles an essayist can play, as envisioned by White in the "Foreword" to his collected essays: "he can pull on any sort of shirt, be any sort of person, according to his mood or his subject matter—philosopher, scold, jester, raconteur, confidante, pundit, devil's advocate, enthusiast." Though I don't have so many personae in my portfolio, the pieces that follow embody some of the different selves that various essayists and issues have called forth in me. Sometimes academic, sometimes playful, sometimes contentious, sometimes intensely personal, I make my way from one essay to the next. So, the book as a whole enacts its concern with the made-up self and the varied ways it can come to life in the work of a single essayist.

I

Evocations of Consciousness

MONTAIGNE ON "MONTAIGNE"

Toward a Poetics of Self

In 1580, Montaigne prefaced the second edition of his essays with the announcement that "I am myself the matter of my book," a commonplace in the twenty-first century, given the current popularity of memoir and the personal essay, but virtually unprecedented in the late sixteenth century, when nonfiction prose was rarely self-referential much less self-absorbed. Equally bold was his prefatory assertion that "I want to be seen here in my simple, natural, ordinary fashion, without straining or artifice, for it is myself that I portray." Given such a declaration of independence from the traditions of classical rhetoric and medieval scholasticism, one might suppose that Montaigne pursued his self-regarding project with utter self-confidence, especially given the bravado of his later assertion in "Of Repentance" that while "Authors communicate with people by some special extrinsic mark: I am the first to do so by my entire being, as Michel de Montaigne, not as a grammarian or a poet or a jurist." But Montaigne's project was so complicated by his idea of the self, which he equated with his thoughts more than with any other dimension of his being, that in twenty-six of his 107 essays he digressed from the subject at hand to ruminate on the problems of reflecting his thoughts in writing. Some of these self-reflexive passages run on for several hundred words, occasionally interrupting an essay five or six times, often expanding in length with each successive edition of his work — digressiveness that provoked Montaigne in his final essay, "Of Experience," to exclaim "How often and perhaps how stupidly have I extended my book to make it speak of itself!" Contrary to his dismay, Montaigne's digressions collectively embody the most detailed and substantial concern with the evocation of consciousness in the history of the personal essay. Such a venturesome concern with the rendering of interiority that it might well be seen as prefiguring modernist evocations of consciousness in the fiction of Woolf and Joyce.

As Montaigne suggests in "Of Practice," his commitment to self-portraiture involved him in the difficult, if not impossible, task of giving visible form to something that is invisible and doing so in the "airy medium" of language: "What I chiefly portray is my cogitations, a shapeless subject that does not lend itself to expression in actions. It is all I can do to couch my thoughts in this airy medium of words." Even more challenging was Montaigne's belief that the self is reflected not just in thoughts per se but in the flow of thought, in the process of meditation and reflection. To portray himself, in other words, required not just an exposition of his thoughts but a depiction of his mind in the process of thinking. For Montaigne, then, the ultimate challenge, as he explained in "Of Practice," was to convey the experience of thinking itself: "It is a thorny undertaking, and more so than it seems, to follow a movement so wandering as that of our minds, to penetrate the opaque depths of its innermost folds, to pick out and immobilize the innumerable flutterings that agitate it." As he defines the problem here, it is caused in part by the inherently digressive habit of the mind, which he depicts as being so dynamic in its "wandering," so given to "movement," to "innumerable flutterings," that "to follow" it would indeed be "a thorny undertaking." Moreover, his final metaphor suggests that the thorniness is caused by attempting not only to track the flow of one's thought but also record the flow and thus "immobilize" it at the very same time that one is immersed in the process of thinking —a cognitive juggling act that is logically impossible without a radical division of one's consciousness into subject and object, into the observer and the thing observed.

Given his commitment to this dizzying mental task, Montaigne evidently went to extraordinary lengths to devise a way of generating his essays that would leave his mind free to follow its own inclinations, as he explains in "Of Books": "As my fancies present themselves, I pile them up; now they come pressing in a crowd, now dragging single file. I want people to see my natural and ordinary pace, however off the track it is." Here as in other passages, Montaigne's composing process appears to be free from any kind of artificial manipulation or intervention, in keeping with his prefatory tribute to the "sweet freedom of nature's first laws." Voicing such convictions, he often sounds like contemporary composition specialists, espousing the principles of free writing. Montaigne was so eager to let his mind follow its natural bent, to include all of its ramblings, that he refused to make any kind of correction, lest he exclude "the imperfections that are ordinary and constant in me." In fact, he was so committed to being seen in his "simple, natural, ordinary fashion" that in "A Consideration upon Cicero" he claimed to "pile up only the headings of subjects," rather than obliging himself to develop them into "numberless essays."

Likewise, in his essay on Virgil, he notes that "when I write, I prefer to do without the company and remembrance of books, for fear they may interfere with my style. Also because, in truth, the good authors humble and dishearten me too much." As these comments suggest, Montaigne evidently felt the anxiety of influence, despite having lived in an era before it became a central preoccupation of literary consciousness. In other essays as well, he goes out of his way to make clear that he quotes others not as authority but as a means of self-expression: "I do not speak the minds of others except to speak my own mind better." Thus Montaigne bears witness to the struggle he went through in trying to convey his own ideas, to be true to his own train of thought, while also being conscious of how deeply influenced he was by his extensive reading.

Much as he sought an uninhibited composing process, Montaigne also proclaims his prose to be free from any mechanical or methodical constraints — "My style and my mind alike go roaming." In keeping with this image of a style in unison with his mind, Montaigne often characterizes his prose as being natural, simple, ordinary, plain, or free, rather than artificial, affected, pedantic, studied, or strained. And as if to heighten the contrast, he tends to use more extreme adjectives and figures in his later essays, referring to his style as crude, harsh, disjointed, imperfect, or undisciplined and to traditional writing as even, orderly, polished, and smooth. For similar reasons, he refuses to be distracted by the bother of correcting his spelling and punctuation.

Just as he disclaims any polish in his style, so in his final essay, "Of Experience," he disavows any structure in his essays or in his work as a whole: "The scholars distinguish and mark off their ideas more specifically and in detail. I, who cannot see beyond what I have learned from experience, without any system, present my ideas in a general way, and tentatively. As in this: I speak my meaning in disjointed parts, as something that cannot be said all at once and in a lump." Here as elsewhere, Montaigne contrasts his work with the methodical discourse of classical rhetoric and medieval scholasticism, and to reinforce the difference he directly expresses his impatience with Cicero's "way of writing, and every other similar way," with "his prefaces, definitions, partitions, etymologies," claiming that "these logical and Aristotelian arrangements are not to the point." Montaigne's objections to such highly formalistic "arrangements" were occasioned not only by a desire to be seen in his "simple, natural, ordinary fashion" but also by an awareness that methodical discourse was expressive of a mental certitude that he did not possess—"If my mind could gain a firm footing, I would not make essays, I would make decisions; but it is always in apprenticeship and on trial."

By pitting himself so clearly and persistently against Aristotle, Cicero, and the medieval scholastics, Montaigne established the now conventional posture of the personal essayist as an independent, often skeptical, mind, exploring ideas and experience outside the confines of received or prevailing intellectual structures. So, too, he established the personal essay as an anti-genre, as an open form of writing, at odds with systematized bodies of knowledge and systematized modes of transmitting knowledge, as he makes clear in this passage from his essay on Virgil: "Learning treats of things too subtly, in a mode too artificial and different from the common and natural one. . . . If I were of the trade, I would naturalize art as much as they artify nature."

But even in the act of staking out a libertarian role for himself, Montaigne was evidently quite conscious that his composing process and his prose were not so free and natural as they might seem. As early as the first edition, he acknowledged in "Of Presumption" that "I am quite conscious that sometimes I let myself go too far, and that in the effort to avoid art and affection, I fall back into them in another direction." By the second edition, he openly admitted that his way of writing is deliberately calculated to create the illusion of being a free and natural activity:

> I go out of my way, but rather by license than carelessness. My
> ideas follow one another, but sometimes it is from a distance,

and look at each other, but with a sidelong glance. I have run my eyes over a certain dialogue of Plato, a fantastic motley in two parts, the beginning part about love, all the rest about rhetoric. The ancients do not fear these changes, and with wonderful grace they let themselves thus be tossed in the wind, or seem to. The titles of my chapters do not always embrace their matter; often they only denote it by some sign like those other titles, "The Maid of Andros," "The Eunuch," or those other names, Sulla, Cicero, Torquatus. I love the poetic gait by leaps and gambols. It is an art, as Plato says, light, flighty, daemonic. There are works of Plutarch's in which he forgets his theme, in which the treatment of his subject is quite smothered in foreign matter. See his movements in "The Daemon of Socrates." Lord, what beauty there is in these lusty sallies and this variation, and more so the more casual and accidental they seem. It is the inattentive reader who loses my subject, not I. Some word about it will always be found in a corner, which will not fail to be sufficient, though it takes little room. I seek out change indiscriminately and tumultuously. My style and my mind alike go roaming.

Throughout this notable passage from "Of Vanity," Montaigne seeks to dispel the impression that his essays are the product of undisciplined thinking and writing. So, while he begins by acknowledging his digressive tendencies, he insists that they are the product of "license [rather] than carelessness," of deliberateness rather than chance, of art rather than nature. Montaigne is so concerned here to distinguish his intentional digressiveness from authorial carelessness that he devotes the rest of the passage to defining and explaining a revolutionary concept of textual coherence which accounts for the unity of his work. He defines this concept in the second sentence, by means of an arresting personification which endows his "ideas" with the capacity to "follow one another, but . . . from a distance, and look at each other, but with a sidelong glance." As this personification suggests, Montaigne conceives of his ideas as being so deeply allied to each other that their inner cohesiveness has the power to overcome the surface digressiveness of his prose. Having defined his special theory of coherence, Montaigne cites the classical precedents for it in Plato's *Phaedrus* and Plutarch's

"The Daemon of Socrates," carefully drawing out the parallels between these works and his own by noting that "the ancients . . . let themselves . . . be tossed in the wind, or seem to."

Montaigne's repeated concern with a calculatedly wrought impression of digressiveness reaches its climax at the end of the first paragraph in his exclamatory transformation of the concept into an esthetic principle — "Lord what beauty there is in these lusty sallies and this variation, and more so the more casual and accidental they seem." In this bold exclamation, Montaigne openly espouses a policy not of naturalness but of studied casualness or, to be more exact, of artful artlessness. Indeed, in the paragraph immediately following this exclamation, he declares that "it is the inattentive reader who loses my subject not I. Some word about it will always be found off in a corner, which will not fail to be sufficient, though it takes little room." Thus, Montaigne depicts his essays as the outcome of a complex mental balancing act, in which he lets his thoughts wander freely enough so that they seem to be "casual" and "accidental" yet keeps them sufficiently controlled so that they do "follow one another," no matter how superficially disconnected they may seem to be. He conceives of his writing, then, as being at once the embodiment and the enactment of a mind freely following its own changeable directions — a paradoxical conception that is echoed by personal essayists as varied as Gass, Gerould, Hardwick, Hoagland, Kazin, and White.

Given this conception of his essays, Montaigne recognized that they call for a correspondingly radical approach to reading and interpretation, the nature of which he insinuates throughout the previous passage. For example, in discussing both his essays and their classical precedents, he focuses attention on aspects of their form that defy the conventional expectations of readers, such as chapter titles that "do not always embrace their matter," abrupt "changes" in "subject" from one part of a piece to the next or even from one sentence to the next, and statements of "theme" that can be "found only incidentally, quite smothered in foreign matter . . . off in a corner, which will not fail to be sufficient, though it takes little room." Elsewhere in a similar vein, he acknowledges that his essays are filled with "stories" and "quotations" that "often bear, outside of my subject, the seeds of a richer and bolder material, and sound obliquely a subtler note, both for myself, who do not wish to express anything more, and for those who get my drift." But Montaigne also recognized that digressive or unrelated material is likely to confound an "inattentive reader," especially one accustomed to methodically written texts that contain "links and seams introduced for the benefit of weak or heedless ears." His essays, in other words, cannot be literally interpreted, because they do not assert their meaning in the forthright and systematic ways that characterize rhetorical and scholastic discourse. Indeed, given their allusive, digressive, and disjunctive form, his essays require instead an attentive reader, attuned to following all of his mental jaunts, a reader who like him "loves the poetic gait, by leaps and gambols." By positing such a reader, Montaigne deftly allies the personal essay with texts that use language imaginatively and thus require literary rather than literal interpretation.

The need for such interpretation is especially true of Montaigne's comments about the subjectivity of his work. Most of these widely scattered comments echo his prefatory desire "to be seen here in my simple, natural, ordinary fashion, without straining or artifice, for it is myself that I portray." So one can easily be lulled into taking them at face value, as reiterations of his self-regarding purpose and persona. But from one passage to the next, Montaigne tends to invoke different metaphors or definitions in discussing the reflexivity of his work, as if he were trying out different ways of expressing the relationship between his essays and himself. So, it seems appropriate to examine these passages in detail, not only because they directly address what Montaigne claimed to be the hallmark of his essays but also because they tacitly explore the relationship of the persona to the essayist's self.

In some passages, Montaigne depicts his essays as being so intimately connected to himself and authentically expressive of himself as to be indistinguishable from himself, indeed, identical with himself, as he asserts in "Of Repentance": "In other cases, one may commend the work apart from the workman; not so here; he who touches the one touches the other." By equating his book and himself in such emphatic terms, Montaigne confers upon each the qualities of the other. To read his essays, then, is to partake of his essential being—his "cogitations"—as surely as if one were literally in his presence or, for that matter, in the presence of his mind itself; and to be in his presence is presumably to partake of his book as surely as if one were literally reading his essays—"he who touches the one touches the other." But in other statements, clearly at odds with such a striking equation, Montaigne portrays his writing as being in some sense distinctly different from himself, a difference resulting from what appears to be an unavoidable obedience to the rules and etiquette of public discourse: "There is no description equal in difficulty, or certainly in usefulness to the description of oneself. Even so one must spruce up, even so one must present one-self in an orderly arrangement, if one would go out in public. Now, I am constantly adorning myself, for I am constantly describing my-self."

In this passage from "Of Practice," as in his prefatory note, Montaigne acknowledges the necessity to "spruce up" before going "out in public," so it might seem at first that he is simply referring to the act of editing his thoughts to fit the rules of public taste. But by this point it should be clear from his preoccupation with the natural flow of his thoughts that he is ultimately concerned with the manipulation or distortion of the flow that inevitably arises from the exigency of having to put one's thoughts in a publicly intelligible form—"in an orderly arrangement, if one would go out in public." These phrases seem to imply that the movement from inner speech to written text results in the creation of a persona that is in some respects dissimilar from the flow of his thought and thereby from an inner sense of himself. And thus in the final sentence of the passage he metaphorically portrays the discrepancy between his writing and his thinking, between his book and himself, as being an inexorable and interminable state of affairs—"I am constantly adorning myself, for I am constantly describing myself."

This difference, as Montaigne makes clear, also arises from the intimate relationship between himself and his work, a relationship that paradoxically divides them even as it ties them to one another, much as a parent and child inescapably grow apart from each other despite their manifold ties to each other:

> To this child, such as it is, what I give I give purely and irrev-
> ocably, as one gives to the children of one's body. The little
> good I have done for it is no longer at my disposal. It may know
> a good many things that I no longer know and hold from me
> what I have not retained and what, just like a stranger, I should

have to borrow from it, if I came to need it. If I am wiser than it, it is richer than I.

In this touching passage from "Of the Affection of Fathers for Their Children," Montaigne conveys the painful distance that has already developed between himself and his work, though the work is still in progress, a distance so great that he looks upon his book as being "like a stranger." That distance, as his metaphor suggests, is the ineluctable consequence of changes that Montaigne himself has undergone. He is, after all, no longer the same person who wrote the essays preceding this passage. His mind is not in possession of, or possessed by, the thoughts that occupy his book. Indeed, he is "wiser" than his work by virtue of being open to experience and change as his book cannot be, no matter how much he might revise it and expand it, while at the same time his book is "richer" than he by virtue of retaining everything with which Montaigne has endowed it, much of which he himself may have forgotten or forsaken.

Given such a clear and evocative assertion of the difference between his work and himself, it seems inconceivable that Montaigne could elsewhere have laid claim to such a close identity between his work and himself. But as if to defy logic, he maintains these two diametrically opposed positions at one point within a single passage:

> In modeling this figure upon myself, I have had to fashion and compose myself so often to bring myself out, that the model itself has to some extent grown firm and taken shape. Painting myself for others, I have painted my inward self with colors clearer than my original ones. I have no more made my book than my book has made me — a book consubstantial with its author, concerned with my own self, an integral part of my life; not concerned with some third-hand, extraneous purpose, like all other books.

In the first two sentences of this passage from "Of Giving the Lie," Montaigne depicts himself as having composed his thoughts so often to make them publicly acceptable and intelligible that he has "painted my inward self with colors clearer than my original ones." These first two sentences suggest that Montaigne thinks of his work as being somehow different from himself. But in the third sentence, he transforms the difference into a source of identity, by means of an arresting turn of thought, in which he conceives of a reciprocal relationship between his essays and himself — "I have no more made my book than my book has made me." By recognizing that the act of writing is doubly formative — that the self is both the shaper and the thing shaped — Montaigne is able not only to resolve the contradiction but also to make the extraordinary claim that his work is "consubstantial with its author." In this striking conceit, as in no other moment in his essays, Montaigne lays claim to a unique, indeed mystical, identity between his book and himself.

This boldly religious metaphor has understandably attracted considerable attention from commentators on Montaigne, so much so that in some cases it has been taken to be a dominant emblem for Montaigne's conception of the relationship between his essays and himself. But the closest that he ever comes elsewhere in the essays to reaffirming the consubtantiality of his book and himself is in the three very brief passages that I have already cited. In other cases, by contrast, he refers to the book quite simply as a "history," "mem-oir," or "record" of his "reveries," "ideas," or "thoughts," and in doing so he tacitly makes a clear distinction between his essays and him-self. In still other cases, he refers to his writing as a "confession," a means of "revealing" himself or of making himself known and thus conceives of it neither as a static record nor as a consubstantial being but as a devout activity. And in yet another set of passages, more numerous and extensive than the others, he refers to his work as a "painting" or "self-portrait." This metaphor, as distinguished from the others, implies that his work constitutes an artistic like-ness, rather than a replication, record, or revelation of his self.

It's tempting to suppose that the idea of self-portraiture was uppermost in Montaigne's thinking, not only because it appears more often than the other metaphors, but also because it involves the epistemological and technical problems of simultaneously ob-serving and portraying oneself that Dürer had already confronted in the visual medium of painting and that was clearly a besetting problem for Montaigne in tracking and transcribing his thoughts. But the metaphor of self-portraiture often appears side by side with one of the others, and over the course of such passages, Montaigne does not give any clear indication as to which metaphor takes pre-cedence. In the passage analyzed above, the metaphor of consubstantiation clearly supersedes that of self-portraiture. But in other cases, Montaigne moves so quickly from one metaphor to the other that he seems to be using them almost interchangeably:

> Others form man; I tell of him and portray a very particular one whom I should make very different from what he is if I had to fashion him over again. But now it is done. Now the lines of my painting do not go astray, though they change and vary. The world is but a perennial movement. All things in it are in constant motion — the earth, the rocks of the Caucasus, the pyramids of Egypt — both with the common motion and with their own. Stability itself is nothing but a more languid motion. I cannot keep my subject still. It goes along befuddled and staggering with a natural drunkenness. I take it in this condition, just as it is at the moment I give my attention to it. I do not portray being: I portray passing. Not the passing from one age to another, or, as the people say, from seven years to seven years, but from day to day, from minute to minute. My history needs to be adapted to the moment. I may presently change, not only by chance, but also by intention. This is a record of various and changeable occurrences, and of irresolute and, when it so befalls, contradictory ideas: whether I am different myself, or whether I take hold of my subjects in different circumstances and aspects. So, all in all, I may indeed contradict myself now and then; but truth, as Demades said, I do not contradict. If my mind could gain a firm footing, I would not make essays, I would make decisions; but it is always in apprenticeship and on trial.

In this well-known passage from the opening of "Of Repentance," Montaigne seems committed at first to the metaphor of self-portraiture, for he announces it at the opening of the first paragraph, returns to it again at the opening of the second, and then builds upon it through the first half of the third paragraph. The image he develops of trying to paint a subject that is continually in motion seems a consummately effective way of suggesting the ambitiousness — and the hopelessness — of trying to convey the incessant flow of his thought. But, as if in keeping with the Heraclitean drift of the passage, he suddenly abandons the metaphor of self-portraiture in mid-paragraph and proceeds to define the exceptional nature of his task by depicting himself as a chronicler attempting to record the history of events that are changing from moment to moment—a task made all the more difficult because he is himself changing from moment to moment. Like expressive variations upon a theme, Montaigne's metaphors reinforce one another here, as he spirals toward the climax of these reflections on the inextricable relationship between the motions of his mind and the movement of his prose—"if my mind could gain a firm footing, I would not make essays, I would make decisions."

Given the restless state of mind that Montaigne acknowledges here and elsewhere, it's hardly surprising that he did not ever settle on a single metaphor or single point of view in reflecting on his essays and himself. At some moments, evidently, he regarded his work as being so faithful a reflection of his mind in action as to be virtually identical, indeed "consubstantial," with himself, or at least to be an authentic revelation and embodiment of himself. At other times, just as obviously, he regarded his book as being more nearly an artistic representation or reconstruction of his thinking and thus referred to it as a portrayal of himself or as a history or record of himself. Though he often wavered among the different metaphors and their differing implications, on some occasions he apparently saw so little difference as to use them interchangeably or to resolve their contradictions by a leap of wit or faith. Ultimately, Montaigne did not maintain a stable conception of his work and its relationship to himself, except, of course, for his unremitting desire to bring it "to fidelity." In relentlessly pursuing that goal and relentlessly reflecting upon his pursuit of it, Montaigne endowed the personal essay with an intense commitment to tracking and tracing one's inner life—to a consciousness of consciousness that has been, perhaps, its most enduring and definitive quality.

THE MIND AND THE MIND'S IDIOSYNCRASY
Ideas of Consciousness in the Personal Essay

he mind, the mind—it's probably not what first comes to mind when one thinks about the personal essay, but it's certainly on the mind of essayists who write about it. Montaigne made it a leitmotif of his essays, cogitating so often upon the nature of his cogitations as to endow his work with a profoundly self-reflexive cast. And one can readily hear echoes of Montaigne's preoccupation in essayists of our own time. In Katherine Gerould's belief that "An essay, to some extent, thinks aloud." In Alfred Kazin's disarming assertion that "In an essay, it is not the thought that counts but the experience we get of the writer's thoughts." In Edward Hoagland's conviction that "essays are directly concerned with the mind and the mind's idiosyncrasy." In Elizabeth Hardwick's space-age conception of the essay as "thought itself in orbit." In Cynthia Ozick's humbler description of it as "a stroll through someone's mazy mind." In John D'Agata's assertion that "the essay is the equivalent of a mind in rumination." In Ander Monson's conviction that "stepping into an essay is stepping into the writer's mind." As if the movements of a mind were more compelling than its matter. As if the play of ideas were more important than the ideas themselves. Probably not an agreeable notion to argumentative essayists, rhetorical theorists, or freshman writing instructors. Yet what could be more germane to argument than the workings of a mind in the process of thought? And what could be more profoundly personal, more intimate, than the revelation of a mind in the process of thought? No wonder Montaigne (in a thinly veiled sexual metaphor) sought "to penetrate the opaque depths of its innermost folds." So ambitious an undertaking that in "Emerson and the Essay," William Gass proclaims "the hero of the essay" to be "the author in the act of thinking things out, feeling and finding a way." A notable conceit—the essayist as literary hero—and Gass is not alone in thinking so, given Lopate's assertion in "The Essay Lives—in Disguise" that "the track of a person's thoughts struggling to achieve some understanding of a problem is the plot, is the adventure" of an essay.

Such a concurrence of belief that it sounds like an incontrovertible truth—the personal essay is not just a product of mind, but as Scott Russell Sanders asserts, "the closest thing we have, on paper, to a record of the individual mind at work and play." Process and product all wrapped up in one grand package—so distinctive in its reflection of the mind and the mind's idiosyncrasy as to constitute a unique "branch of literature." The literature of interiority. The story of thought. The drama of mind in action. Thought and the process of thought united in a single text. It's an alluring idea, especially for those of us who consider the personal essay to be as significant and compelling in its own right as fiction, poetry, or drama. Not a servant or second-class citizen in the world of literature. All of which is to say that I'm sorely tempted to affirm that it does, indeed, reveal the mind of the essayist in the process of trying to find what will suffice. But the skeptical side of me wonders how one could possibly make such an inference without being privy to the mind of an essayist (to the minds of many essayists!) in the process of composing an essay. The mind's a fine and private place, but none I think do there embrace.

Even if one could get inside the head of another human being, I have a hunch that its workings would turn out to be far messier than anything in a personal essay, given what's going on right now in my own upstairs. The ceiling fan whirring above my head, the cursor blinking on my screen, both so incessant, so unwavering, they make me wonder why I too cannot maintain such focus. Probably because I'm distracted by the stuffed cabbage that needs to go into the oven in fifteen minutes, and the cucumbers that need harvesting, and the groundhog that ravaged a couple of my broccoli plants this morning. Or by the memory of lunching with Kazin some forty years ago, just about the time he published the textbook anthology that includes his remarks about experiencing an essayist's thought. Too bad I couldn't have foreseen this tête-à-tête either then or some twenty years later when we spent a summer afternoon on my terrace, chatting on this and that. Too bad also that I didn't take more careful notes several years ago when Sanders came to Iowa City and spent an afternoon vividly detailing the elaborate plans and notes that go into the crafting of his evocative essays, as if to refute his own remarks about the essay as "a record of the individual mind at work and play." So many disparate memories and thoughts running through my head—the telephone ringing now in the background, the dog waiting downstairs for his predinner walk—that even these last few sentences are a pale reflection of the muddle that's going on inside. Maybe Kazin and Sanders have more disciplined minds than I. Or maybe they never intended their statements to be taken quite so literally as to posit a one-for-one correspondence between the flow of an essay and the track of an essayist's mind.

And yet. The latitude of the personal essay has just given me the freedom to romp through my attic, my vegetable garden, and my memories of Kazin while trying to negotiate a literary discussion. So it does in a sense reflect the track of my thoughts, "struggling to achieve some understanding of a problem." The track, however, is a contrivance of sorts. Not the thoughts and memories themselves, but my self-conscious decision to include them here as an example of the mind's meanderings, and then to jog my memory for other recollections, and then to work over the sequence, syntax, and wording of those memories and thoughts to suggest the movement of a mind interacting with itself. Seemingly on an associative ramble but with a destination in mind. Seemingly in an extemporaneous style but deliberately revised to create that illusion.

The illusion is the product of a quasi-improvisational art that personal essayists have been practicing ever since Montaigne. Joseph Addison acknowledges the illusion of spontaneity, the seemingly associative quality, when he says that in writing an essay, which he distinguishes from "a Set Discourse," "it is sufficient that I have several Thoughts on a Subject, without troubling my self to range them in such order, that they may seem to grow out of one another." Gass explicitly defines the illusion when he speaks of Emerson as having "made the essay into the narrative disclosure of thought . . . but not of such thinking as had actually occurred. Real thought is gawky and ungracious." Similarly, Lopate notes that the personal essay "seems to lay bare its process as it goes along. I say 'seems' because there is still a good deal of selection and art in this appearance of spontaneous process." Aldous Huxley defines the process as "free association artistically controlled," and Theodor Adorno codifies the paradox in his idea of the essay's "methodical unmethodicality." Monson acknowledges the illusory nature of it all in his definition of the essay as "a simulation of the mind working its way through a problem." Likewise Paul Graham who speaks of it as "a train of thought—but a cleaned up train of thought." No matter how one defines it, the personal essay, according to such essayists, requires a delicate set of mental adjustments, attuned both to giving the mind free rein while also reining it in, so that the essay might appear to be a stroll through someone's mazy mind, but a mind that is always in control of itself no matter how wayward it may seem to be. The mind's idiosyncrasy—or so it would seem.

Why bother? Why all this fuss about the illusion of thought in orbit, about an apparent stroll through someone's mazy mind? Listen to Montaigne in "Of Experience," and it sounds like a skeptic's opposition to the methods and certitudes of scholasticism. A distrust of scholarly method that one can hear again in Gass's antithetical portraits of the academic article and the essay:

> [The article] must appear complete and straightforward and footnoted and useful and certain and is very likely a veritable Michelin of misdirection; for the article pretends that everything is clear, that its argument is unassailable, that there are no soggy patches, no illicit inferences, no illegitimate connections. . . . The essay is unhurried (although Bacon's aren't); it browses among books; it enjoys an idea like a fine wine; it thumbs through things. It turns round and round upon its topic, exposing opinions, disposing of prejudice and even of simple truth itself—as too undeveloped, not yet of an interesting age.

Gass's contrast, which features the essayist thinking things out, struggling with problematic experience, seems to embody a tacit challenge to methodical and dogmatic forms of knowledge and discourse. A philosophical putdown in the form of a personal ramble. A mocking refusal to play the academic game. A dramatic proof of one's freedom from systematized modes of thinking and writing. But listen again to Montaigne, and the illusion sounds like a deliberate aesthetic policy, complete with classical precedents, affirming the beauty of a well-crafted ramble, of an artfully artless run of thought, as if the performance were to be prized for itself alone: "Lord, what beauty there is in these lusty sallies and this variation, and more so the more casual and accidental they seem."

So much enthusiasm for a seemingly accidental digression (in a digression near the end of "Of Vanity") that it makes me think I should ballyhoo the sunflowers blooming along the back of my vegetable bed—bright yellow, yellow-orange, brown and yellow, yellow and purple, purple and black, rust—tossing in the wind, sprouted from the fallen seed of last year's flowers, and the seed from defecating birds, and my own seeding, all so casually arrayed, all so different not only in the color and size of their blossoms but also in the shape of their foliage and the height of their growth, it might not be evident that I thin them to create the impression of a randomly scattered but harmonious bed of variegated blooms. The exact counterpart of the perfectly rectangular dill bed a few feet in front, so thick with umbelliferous heads waving in the breeze it might seem as if I'd carefully scattered the seed to produce that geometric shape, whereas the dill, in fact, has been reseeding itself throughout the garden ever since I first planted it there some thirty years ago, and now I simply craft a shapely plot each year by thinning out all the unwanted seedlings. Dill, anyone?

Sometimes I wonder why I do such things. Why do I now plant flowers and herbs amid my once-sacrosanct vegetable garden? Why such deceptive beds of this and that within its once carefully balanced rows of broccoli at one end, cauliflower at the other, snow peas at one end, shell peas at the other, onions at one end, leeks at the other? Boredom? Rebellion? Experimentation? A delight in disorder among the order? Or a hunger for something like the seemingly random but selective workings of nature itself? Maybe I should stop planting altogether, and let things take their course from all the scattered seeds of all the things I've ever planted. And so produce a fantastic motley, like Montaigne's "Of Vanity"—a twenty-five-thousand word ramble that touches on writing, on death, on travel, on staying put, on household affairs, on friendship, on marriage, on self-sufficiency, on indebtedness, on conscience, on legal obligation, and also occasionally on vanity. No wonder he wryly declares that "the titles of my chapters do not always embrace their matter." It's virtually impossible to take one's bearings in the process of reading a work such as "Of Vanity," for the subject at hand is always changing, as mutable and destabilizing as the ambiguous and shifting perspectives in an M. C. Escher landscape. Oh yes, it begins with a sentence that is clearly on target, "There is perhaps no more obvious vanity than to write of it so vainly." But from then on, the essay so often seems to be concerned with other more pressing subjects that one might well conclude there is no more obvious vanity than to read of it so vainly, especially when one happens to notice the digressive additions that Montaigne has made from one version of the essay to the next.

————

Digression — the rhetorical embodiment of a mind "slipping," as Ozick puts it, "from one impression to another, from reality to memory to dreamscape and back again." Digression — not just an occasional detour signaled in advance by an attentive author but repeated, unanticipated shifts of attention from one subject to another. Frequent enough to create the impression of a consciousness so absorbed by its kaleidoscopic interests as to be almost oblivious of an audience. A mind turned in upon itself. Digression — the rhetorical outcome of free association. So universal a habit of mind that one might consider it a sine qua non of consciousness in the personal essay. What else could have inspired Montaigne to make it a hallmark of his art? What else could possibly create so compelling an illusion of thought in action, of the mind and the mind's idiosyncrasy?

What else, but the antithesis of digression. A consciousness so relentlessly focused upon something as to be oblivious of almost everything else. The tyranny of a single image, idea, memory, or problem — and the compulsion to understand it. A mind in the self-absorbed process of trying to find what will suffice, seeking the grail of insight. Like Annie Dillard's fixation in "Living Like Weasels." Or Joan Didion's tenacious preoccupation in "On Keeping a Notebook," her thoughts set in motion by an intriguingly cryptic note written some five years earlier:

> "'That woman Estelle,'" the note reads, "'is partly the reason why George Sharp and I are separated today.' *Dirty crepe-de-Chine wrapper, hotel bar, Wilmington RR, 9:45 a.m. August Monday morning.*" Since the note is in my notebook, it presumably has some meaning to me. I study it for a long while.

But no sooner does Didion decipher the note, reconstructing the details of that train station episode, than she finds herself troubled by a vexing array of questions: "Why did I write it down? In order to remember, of course, but exactly what was it I wanted to remember? How much of it actually happened? Did any of it? Why do I keep a notebook at all?" Why write, she also might have asked and did so several years later in "Why I Write." But here it's the notebook and why she keeps it that haunt her from start to finish — haunt her so much that she never digresses from that overriding question, relentlessly scouring her notes in search of an answer. Such a single-minded quest that it resonates with the intensity of an existential compulsion: "What is this business about 'shopping, typing piece, dinner with E, depressed'? Shopping for what? Typing what piece? Who is E? Was this 'E' depressed, or was I depressed? Who cares?" Didion cares, and cares so much that she draws one into her caring. And not just by the emotional drive of her persistent questions but by the immediacy of her mental gyrations, her thoughts spinning in present tense around the question of her notebook. In present tense. As if one were inside her head, tracking the movement of her mind, witnessing the flow of her thoughts and counterthoughts, as they emerge:

> How it felt to me: that is getting closer to the truth about
> a notebook. I sometimes delude myself about why I keep a
> notebook, imagine that some thrifty virtue derives from pre-
> serving everything observed. . . . I imagine, in other words, that
> the notebook is about other people. But of course it is not. I
> have no real business with what one stranger said to another at
> the hat-check counter in Pavillon. . . . Remember what it was to
> be me: that is always the point.

Thoughts, of course, do not ordinarily emerge in such polished prose as that. Still, the immediacy of her meditation makes it seem as if I'm listening in on something like an interior dialogue, a conversation between Didion and herself. A probing dialogue that gradually leads to a climactic series of insights about a notebook as the means "to keep on nodding terms with the people we used to be, whether we find them attractive company or not." So her essay is structured somewhat like a personal quest, a solitary struggle to gain some understanding of "the truth about a notebook." And by extension, it seems that the form of her essay, beginning as it does with such an intriguing but puzzling note, is meant to draw me into the struggle as well, as if to suggest that the experience of seeking the truth might be as important as the truth itself. As if the question—and the inquiring mind working its way toward insight—might be as important as the answer. As if Didion had pulled back the screen that veils the inner sanctum of consciousness, enabling one to behold something like a spontaneous run of thought —unmediated, unrevised, uncontrived. The thing itself. Or so it would seem.

But how about a completely different kind of interiority? Not the immediacy of a relentlessly focused quest like Didion's but memory in a flash, a sudden flashback, the kind that sweeps unbidden across the mind and leaves one momentarily dazed. There but not there. A striking manifestation of the mind's capacity to be in two places at once—time present and time past converging in an instant. Yet how can one embody such a transient experience, except perhaps in a manner somewhat like Loren Eiseley's at the beginning of "The Bird and the Machine," where he appears to be completely preoccupied with the fate of some creatures from the past— distracted by a fleeting memory. So preoccupied that he doesn't even bother to identify exactly what he's thinking about until he's suddenly puzzled by the very subject of his preoccupation:

> I suppose their little bones have years ago been lost among the stones and winds of those high glacial pastures. I suppose their feathers blew eventually into the piles of tumbleweed beneath the straggling cattle fences and rotted there in the mountain snows, along with dead steers and all the other things that drift to an end in the corners of the wire. I do not quite know why I should be thinking of birds over the *New York Times* at breakfast, particularly the birds of my youth half a continent away.

Such a disarming way to begin an essay—the subject of Eiseley's thoughts obscured by a vague pronoun reference—that it immediately foregrounds his mental distraction, as if he were completely oblivious of his readers, indifferent to the usual expositional courtesies. "What is this essay about?" one might wonder in the process of reading those first two sentences, but Eiseley doesn't offer much help, not even in the third sentence, when he explicitly refers to "the birds of my youth." For by that point, he seems to be concerned as much with the turn of his thoughts, the track of his memory, as with the fate of those birds. The mind bemused by itself, ruminating upon the mysteries of its movement, as Eiseley does even more explicitly in the next sentence:

> It is a funny thing what the brain will do with memories and how it will treasure them and finally bring them into odd juxtapositions with other things, as though it wanted to make a design, or get some meaning out of them, whether you want it or not, or even see it.

Though it doesn't clarify the drift of his essay, this resonant bit of reflection does suggest that Eiseley, like Hoagland and other essayists, is fascinated by the mind and its manifold abilities—not only to store memories and retrieve them but also to combine them "with other things" in surprising and significant ways. Yet Eiseley's designation of the brain, rather than the mind, as a seemingly autonomous source of such doings, "whether you want it or not, or even see it," suggests that he might also be intrigued by the possibility of a counterpart to the personal essay—a ghostly version of it—predicated on an unconscious, rather than conscious, crafting of memory. A haunting idea that seems to be embodied in the very form and content of Eiseley's essay. For "The Bird and the Machine" certainly does contain an unusual juxtaposition of memories with other things—a mélange that culminates in a vividly detailed recollection of those birds from Eiseley's youth, preceded by another story from the same time, when he was "left alone in a great desert," preceded by reflections on computers, automatons, robots, puppets, and clocks, as well as on "the shape of the future brooding in mice" and on the variable nature of time in different planes of existence—a wide range of irritable musings provoked by an article in his morning newspaper about machines that might replicate the "complicated feedback system of the brain." All of which is to say that "The Bird and the Machine" contains such a strange amalgam of things that it might almost seem to be the unconscious product of Eiseley's brain, wanting "to make a design, or get some meaning out of them." As if Eiseley were an amanuensis of sorts, and the essay a transcription of his brain's unconscious devising. Not literally, of course, but imitatively. A work, in other words, that stands as a compelling emblem of what the human brain can do that's inimitable by machines, much as his memory of a female hawk joyously recovering her mate stands as a powerful reminder that a "machine does not bleed, ache, hang for hours in the empty sky in a torment of hope to learn the fate of another machine, nor does it cry out with joy nor dance in the air with the fierce passion of a bird."

Moving as it is to read of the hawks reconnoitering in the sky, the moment of their reunion is matched by an extraordinary conjunction of time past and time present in Eiseley's memory of the birds:

> Straight out of the sun's eye, where she must have been soaring restlessly above us for untold hours, soared his mate. And from far up, ringing from peak to peak of the summits over us, came a cry of such unutterable and ecstatic joy that it sounds down across the years and tingles among the cups of my breakfast table. I saw them both now. He was rising to meet her.

The first time I read that passage, some thirty years ago, I was so absorbed by the ecstatic reunion of the birds, dramatically narrated by Eiseley in past tense, in rhetorically heightened sentences, that his sudden shift to present tense — in midsentence! — took me completely by surprise. Unexpectedly, my attention had been reoriented from those birds in the backward abysm of time to the immediacy of Eiseley at his breakfast table, seeing the birds once again. As if his narrative recollection had inadvertently given rise to a virtual re-perception of the birds. A self-induced flashback of sorts, thanks to the magic of mind — magic that Eiseley tacitly celebrates throughout the essay and dramatically displays in that climactic episode.

———

This morning, the first day of spring, I looked out the kitchen windows and noticed a red-tailed hawk, riding the thermals in a patch of sky above the neighborhood park. But I didn't see another hawk rising to meet it in midair, though I gazed out the windows for several minutes, until the waffle iron started smoking in the background. Too much of a coincidence to hope for, even in this season of mating birds. And what if I had seen a pair of hawks converging in our neighborhood sky? Would they have stuck in my mind or moved me as much as those birds in Eiseley's essay? Could I ever have thought of them apart from their connection to those birds of Eiseley's youth? It's a funny thing how someone's written memory can have more staying power than your own firsthand observation—can stick in your mind together with other recollections and shape the way you think about things whether you know it or not. It helps, of course, if the writer has a good story and a good memory for details, as Eiseley clearly does in his vivid account of the hawks. But compelling as it is, that story, like Eiseley's recollection of his months in the desert, is so deeply permeated by his brooding consciousness that the essay as a whole ultimately seems animated much more by the arresting movements of his mind than the sentience of those birds and the strange tempo of desert life. In fact, whenever I think of Eiseley's piece, it's his preoccupied musing at the start and his surprising flashback near the end that immediately come to mind, much as the first things that come to mind when I think of Didion's piece are the immediacy and persistence of her self-probing questions.

Sometimes I wonder if I'm just a sucker for such special effects, such dramatic emblems of the mind's idiosyncrasy. But then it occurs to me that the significance of memories and thoughts—like the import of dreams—is inseparable from the form in which they arise and the mental context in which they take shape. Those "odd juxtapositions" that Eiseley speaks of do, after all, "make a design," make meaning—out of birds, notebooks, newspapers, desert rattlesnakes, abandoned cabins, and anything else that comes to mind from the ebb and flow of experience. So at last it seems all the more important and illuminating to behold the otherwise veiled workings of an essayist's mind. And that leads me to think that perhaps the intense dedication of Montaigne, Didion, Eiseley, and other personal essayists to displaying the drama of thought, the twists and turns of consciousness, might imply that there's something more compelling at stake for them too. Something like an overwhelming desire to recapture, relive, and share those heightened moments of being that arise during a distinctive run of thought, a compelling memory, or a flash of special insight. Moments so fraught with significance yet so fleeting that they seem all the more precious. Like a red-tailed hawk, riding the thermals in a patch of sky above a neighborhood park.

"Anne Carol Moore of the New York Public Library"? Who is she, and why did she write him a letter about being visited by "a representative from Superman, Inc."? And what, pray tell, does a letter about someone from Superman, Inc., whatever that is, have to do with making maple syrup, or maple syrup with tending a brooder stove for young chicks? Talk about a muddle of things—this is certainly it!

It's 1963, and I've just been puzzling over something called "Spring," by E. B. White. I refer to it as "something," because I don't know what to call it or how to describe it. All I know is that it doesn't look like an essay and doesn't read like one, though it's included in *One Man's Meat* together with "Once More to the Lake" and other essays that White wrote for his monthly column in *Harper's* some twenty years earlier. By contrast with those pieces, this one looks like something from another planet. It has twelve segments, typographically separated from each other by asterisks and interspacing. The segments range in length from a sixteen-word sentence fragment at the start to a four-paragraph story and meditation at the end. Some of its interior segments are just a sentence long, others contain three or four sentences, and a couple include three ample paragraphs. Casting my eye over the whole thing, I notice that most of the shorter segments come near the beginning, and a couple of the longer ones come at the end. Beyond that, I don't see any pattern in White's arrangement of them. Nor do I know what to make of the fact that each segment is distinctly different not just in length but in content—a different point of interest in each case. One tells about a letter that White received from Anne Carol Moore of the New York Public Library, describing a visit from "a representative of Superman, Inc."; another about maple syrup "operations," conducted by White's son; the next recalls a conversation with one of White's friends who scornfully advises him "to spare the reading public your little adventures in contentment"; and the next tells about the difficulties of "tending a brooder stove" for 254 "mothering chicks." No wonder I'm a bit puzzled by the piece. But I'm beginning to see that it seems to focus on the joys of spring, also the horrors of war and the necessity to keep writing, no matter what. Yet I don't know why it's written in such disparate segments, in discontinuous form. No sense of continuity except that all the segments deal with things that White experienced or thought about during April 1941, when he was writing the piece for his monthly column.

In contrast with the work as a whole, one of its three-paragraph segments offers such an exquisitely unified description of "the day of days when spring at last" arrives that it could well stand on its own as a self-contained little essay or sketch. In fact, I remember having seen it anthologized as a free-standing essay before I encountered it here within the twelve-segment piece. I remember assigning it some five years before in a freshman writing course, without realizing that it was part of a larger work. Given White's ability to produce such a well-wrought essay about the advent of spring, so lyrical and so artfully developed, I wonder why he's chosen to write such a fragmented work on the subject. I wonder too what could possibly have moved him to write such a disparate set of bits and pieces about life at his saltwater farm — the sort of thing one might produce in a rambling letter to a friend or relative but certainly not in a column for *Harper's*.

————

No, I've not been playing dumb in my reactions to White's piece. I'm simply trying to remember what it was like to confront such a work back in 1963, when traditionally structured forms of the essay and nonfiction were still largely unchallenged. No one then would have been likely to conceive much less produce such a tour de force in discontinuous form as George Trow's provocative essay, *The Harvard Black Rock Forest*, or the edgy portrait embodied in Janet Malcolm's *41 False Starts*, or the lyric essays in John D'Agata's *Halls of Fame*, or Maggie Nelson's *Bluets*, comprised of 240 numbered segments, meditating on the color blue, or David Shields's *Reality Hunger*, a literary manifesto consisting of 617 numbered segments. New Journalism, after all, was just emerging with the publication of Tom Wolfe's "Kandy-Kolored, Tangerine-Flake Streamline Baby," and more than ten years were yet to pass before Wolfe attempted to codify its practices in *The New Journalism*, before Winston Weathers expounded them for teachers of writing in *An Alternate Style: New Options for Composition*, and before John McPhee produced his hauntingly discontinuous piece, "The Search for Marvin Gardens." So when I first encountered White's essay, I didn't have any familiar concepts, categories, or terms, such as "collage" and "crot," with which to understand it. I looked upon it simply as a disparate set of observations and reflections, bearing witness to the drift of White's thoughts, a piece somewhat in the manner of a journal or notebook, for that is how he invited me to see it in the opening segment: "Notes on springtime and on anything else that comes to mind of an intoxicating nature."

It didn't occur to me back then that such a nonchalant fragment might be a pose of sorts, as if to suggest that White is giving us his thoughts exactly as they came to mind, without any revision or stylistic polish. As calculated a stance as Montaigne's assurance that "I let my thoughts run on . . . as I have produced them, without plastering and sewing up the flaws." Except, of course, that he kept revising his essays to create an improvisational effect, much as I've rewritten this piece to undo the tightly interconnected form in which it was first published some fifteen years ago, so that it might seem as if I'm taking things up as they come to mind, without a concern for smooth transitions from one section to the next. Discontinuous form is, after all, not just a mode of presentation but also a means of self-projection. An emblematic type of behavior. I am the form in which I am manifest. Look at me leap from this to that.

"Collage"—it's now the most widely used term for describing the form of such a piece as White's. But I've never been very comfortable with that metaphor. It may, in fact, be a misnomer, a faulty analogy turned into a misleading category. Collage, after all, is a type of visual art, created by Picasso in 1912, when he pasted a piece of commercially printed oilcloth onto the canvas of a work called "Still Life with Chair Caning." In subsequent works, Picasso and Braque used fragments of newspaper, bits of musical notation, segments of printed letters, and other materials to represent different planes, textures, and layers of reality in a cubist composition. Hardly comparable to the free-standing pieces of intelligible prose that figure in a segmented essay. Then the dadaists and surrealists put the technique to use in works made out of incongruously related figures and images cut from engravings, photographs, and printed illustrations. Then, of course, as with most artistic developments, the world of advertising got hold of the technique, and eventually it became an activity for children's art classes.

I remember studying collage during the late-fifties as a teaching assistant in a modern art course. I remember my kids showing me the collages they made at school during the mid-sixties. I remember seeing an exhibit of hauntingly surrealistic collages by a European artist name Esteban Xeros, who turned out to be a hoax created by the Jewish Museum director Alan Solomon. Such intensely visual memories make me uneasy whenever I hear someone using the word collage to describe an essay such as White's "Spring." But it's not just memories that make me uneasy. Substantial differences are at work that make the analogy profoundly misleading.

In fabricating a collage, an artist usually incorporates material from a variety of different sources, reassembling the fragments within an entirely new and different visual construct. An essayist, by contrast, generates most or all of the material that appears in the separate parts of a discontinuous piece. The artist's collage is made of bits and pieces that are inherently meaningless—paper, oilcloth, textiles, string, and so on—whereas a segmented essay is composed of prose passages, every one of which, no matter how different from the others, is intelligible in and of itself. The fragments of a collage are usually mounted on a surface so that they closely adjoin or overlap each other and thus tend to merge into a single image, whereas blocks of prose in a discontinuous essay are spatially marked off from each other, so that rather than merging they retain a distinct separateness from each other. The pieces that make up a collage may, of course, be examined separately; the eye may roam back and forth among them to examine how they have been arranged and affixed in relation to each other; but the collective image tends to exert a powerful hold over one's visual perception and mental conception of the piece, because the whole of it is immediately perceptible. By contrast, the serial arrangement of pieces in a discontinuous essay results in a composition the whole of which can only be taken in gradually and therefore can only be held entirely in mind by a special act of will. Indeed, the fragmented mode of presentation tacitly invites one to consider each segment in and of itself, in relation to every other segment and in relation to the entire set of pieces, resulting in a complex network of understandings gradually arrived at rather than a whole work immediately perceived. Thus collage involves a completely different method of creation from the one that produces a discontinuous essay, and these differing methods yield strikingly different kinds of composition that are perceived in radically different ways.

One thing suggests another, and suddenly I'm thinking about montage — a different kind of cut and paste, entailing a set of discrete images, edited and arranged to produce a distinctive sequential experience. George Orwell's "Marrakech" comes immediately to mind, given its sequence of five visually striking segments, each focused on a different scene in Marrakech and the surrounding countryside, each bearing witness to the dehumanizing influence of a colonial situation. Also Alice Walker's "Beauty: When the Other Dancer Is the Self," each of its eight segments focused on a separate incident in her life, from childhood when she lost the sight of one eye to adulthood when she became reconciled to that loss. Also Vivian Gornick's "On the Street," most of its twelve segments focused on different streets and street scenes in Manhattan. Also David Foster Wallace's "Ticket to the Fair," each of its twenty-four segments focused on a separate moment in his vividly detailed tour of the Illinois State Fair. In each case, a series of arresting snapshots accumulate like separate scenes in a filmic montage to produce a complex impression of place and person. But discontinuous essays are not always so preponderantly scenic as Orwell's or so predominantly narrative as Walker's or so heavily descriptive as Gornick's or so relentlessly chronological and descriptive as Wallace's. So, after all, the analogy to montage doesn't take account of pieces that are primarily reflective, such as Didion's "On Keeping a Notebook," Oates's "Against Nature," Trudy Dittmar's "Paedomorph Pools and Other Blighted Bounties," or Susan Griffin's "Red Shoes." Whatever kind of material is involved, the spatial and typographical separation of segments in such an essay produces the repeated experience of discontinuity, whereas the splicing of shots in a montage produces a sequence that runs uninterruptedly, whether the transitions are smooth or abrupt, match-cut or jump-cut. A quick succession of images is at the heart of montage, whereas an intermittent sequence of recollections and reflections is at work in a discontinuous essay.

———

"Discontinuous"—it works so well to denote the visible and substantive breaks in a segmented piece that it seems to be the most accurate descriptive term. But it might have negative connotations—like many words beginning with "dis-"—, so I've been pondering a more neutral term, such as "paratactic," from the Greek "parataxis," which refers to the placement of clauses or phrases side by side without any type of conjunction. As in, "I came. I saw. I conquered." Or closer to home, "She sits motionless, her eyes fixed on the TV screen. The weather reporter predicts warmer temperatures for next week. I think of the spring vegetables that need to be planted before leaving for New York." By analogy, a "paratactic essay" might be thought of as juxtaposing discrete sentences, paragraphs, and larger units of discourse. Though it's hardly so chic and culturally relevant a term as "collage," parataxis is certainly more akin to what happens in essays such as Orwell's "Marrakech," White's "Spring," Dillard's "Living Like Weasels," and Oates's "My Father, My Fiction," all of which contain discrete sentences, paragraphs, or larger units of discourse placed side by side without any connective or transitional material between them. But "paratactic" is so rarified and antique that it would never have a chance except in highly specialized discourse.

Everyone knows what's involved in the form of such a piece, whether it's called a collage essay, a paratactic essay, or something else altogether, like a patchwork essay, a quilted essay, a lyric essay, or an essay in discontinuous form. None of them is exact. They're all approximations of a sort, metaphors for a kind of essay that's too complex to grasp in a single word. Still, some metaphors are not just more accurate than others. Some are also more suggestive and illuminating. Parataxis, for example, reminds me that discontinuous prose is by no means a contemporary invention, that it has, in fact, a long history, rooted in aspects of classical discourse and style that influenced Montaigne and Bacon. In Bacon, it's immediately evident in an abrupt movement from one aphorism to the next, each as distinctly turned, each as distinctly set off from the others as possible, even to the extent of being typographically marked with paragraph symbols before each aphorism in the 1597 edition of his essays. In Montaigne, abrupt shifts of focus take place between larger blocks of material, so that at one moment he might be telling at length about a nearly fatal accident and in the next reflecting on the usefulness and originality of his writing, as in "Of Practice."

Not only do Bacon and Montaigne write discontinuous essays, they also explain their reasons for doing so in comments indicating that they prize it as a reflection of the fragmentary manner in which thoughts come to mind or suddenly change direction. Bacon, for example, speaks of his essays as "dispersed meditations," "fragments of my conceits," and in *The Advancement of Learning* he defends the aphoristic style as an echo of the disconnected form in which thoughts first arise in the mind. In "Of Vanity," Montaigne offers an extended and exuberant rationale for his use of discontinuous form, climaxed by his exclamation — "Lord, what beauty there is in these lusty sallies and variations, and more so the more casual and accidental they seem."

How can one determine when a leap of thought seems more casual and accidental? Montaigne, alas, doesn't explain. But I suppose it has something to do with the manner of the leap rather than its substance — with wording and phrasing — so that it seems as unassuming, say, as Annie Dillard's remark that "I would like to learn, or remember, how to live," which comes immediately after a segment detailing her confrontation with a weasel. I wonder what I'd be thinking face to face with a weasel. Whatever my thoughts, they'd probably come in fits and starts, as things usually come to mind. In disconnected form. Which reminds me that a segmented piece such as Dillard's or White's might well be understood not just as a record of experience but also as an embodiment of thought. I don't mean to imply that every such essay is an enactment of thought, nor do I mean to suggest that discontinuous form has not or cannot be used for other expressive purposes, such as the evocation of cultural or social fragmentation. But it often does seem to be occasioned at least in part by an impulse to convey a sense of the rich array (one might even say, the disarray) of images, recollections, and reflections that often come to mind during the process of thinking about a particular subject or experience. Some essayists explicitly call attention to the variegated subject matter of their discontinuous pieces, as White does in the opening segment of "Spring" by promising "notes" not only "on springtime" but also "on anything else that comes to mind of an intoxicating nature"; or as Eiseley does in "The Bird and the Machine," reflecting on "what the brain will do with memories and how it will . . . bring them into odd juxtapositions"; or as Woody Allen does in the title of his essay, "Random Reflections of a Second-Rate Mind." But even without such explicit self-referential statements, the segmented form and shifting focus of discontinuous essays tend to suggest the wide-ranging movement of a mind in the process of pondering a particular subject or experience.

White's "Spring" is a case in point, for one can hardly read through its abrupt changes in topic and focus without sensing the instability not only of the season but also of White's thoughts and feelings. In one segment, he worries about the condition of his hog; but a few segments later, after sarcastically reflecting on the representative of Superman, Inc., then painfully recalling the experience of reading *Little Women* during the winter of 1940–41, he exults in "the intoxication" of his young lambs; yet the next segment finds him fretful again, this time about not yet having seen a snake—a harbinger of spring; while in the next segment he notes with pleasure that a pair of starlings are renovating the knothole in a tree on his front lawn. Somewhat later in these mixed impressions, White is deeply troubled by news about the war and by his own lack of involvement in it—"everybody else fighting or dying or working for a cause or writing to his senator, and me looking after some Barred Rock chickens." But no sooner does he worry about indulging himself in a "dreamlike unreality" than he justifies his behavior by flatly asserting that "the land, and the creatures that go with it, are what is left that is good, and they are the authors of the book that I find worth reading."

The discontinuities of a mind in the process of recollection and reflection may also be found in segmented essays that focus on a single topic or experience. In the seven segments of "My Father, My Fiction," Oates moves abruptly amid a wide range of familial information, childhood and adult memories, personal journals, literary and musical texts in an effort to understand one of the central mysteries in her life. And the restlessness of her thoughts is suggested by the occasional moments in which she suddenly steps back to reflect on the process of her pondering and writing: "I wonder if it is evident how painfully difficult it has been for me to write this seemingly informal memoir?—as if I were staring into a dazzling beacon of light, yet expected to see." Such abrupt shifts and striking juxtapositions inevitably produce in me a strange reading experience, unlike that produced by any other kind of prose. Each segment, by virtue of its separateness and distinctiveness, calls upon me to read it and respond to it in and of itself. Yet each segment, by virtue of being only one in a series of other segments, compels me to read it and respond to it in connection with the others, and not just those that immediately precede and follow it but also those that come much earlier or later in the set. Thus in reading a discontinuous essay, I inevitably find myself experiencing at some point an irresolvable tension between two different ways of reading and responding. Early on in my reading, I can easily do justice to each segment both as a discrete entity and in connection with its immediate neighbor. But as I move further into the text my accumulating sense of recurrent or contrastive phrases, images, metaphors, ideas, or themes makes it increasingly difficult to perceive the later segments in and of themselves.

Discontinuous form sometimes embodies not just the abrupt shifts of a mind in the process of recollection and reflection but also the tensions within a mind unable or unwilling to formulate explicit connections among its varied memories and perceptions or resolve contradictions among its varied attitudes, thoughts, and feelings. In "The White Album," Joan Didion made a striking and memorable connection of this sort between discontinuous form and the disconnected state of her own perceptions:

> I was meant to know the plot, but all I knew was what I saw: flash pictures in variable sequence, images with no meaning beyond their temporary arrangement, not a movie but a cutting-room experience. In what would probably be the middle of my life I wanted still to believe in the narrative and in the narrative's intelligibility, but to know that one could change the sense with every cut was to begin to perceive the experience as rather more electrical than ethical.

But Didion so clearly associated the segmented form of that well-known essay—the "cutting-room" quality of it—with her own mental breakdown and a breakdown in the culture that the discontinuous essay has often been regarded primarily as an emblem of the post-sixties or postmodern visions of a self or a world fragmented beyond reclamation. And since then, of course, it has often been used for just such purposes.

But I also believe that discontinuous form has been the outgrowth of a profound skepticism about the possibility of universal knowledge or the permanence of any reality except the reality of change and the uncertainty born of such change. Montaigne, of course, is the earliest and most well-known essayist to endow it with such philosophical significance. Yet it is striking to note the wide range of essayists who have also chosen to "speak in disjointed parts" for similarly philosophical reasons—reasons that have motivated them, like Montaigne, to conceive of the essay itself as being inherently disjointed and thereby a direct challenge to academic and other institutionally systematized forms of thought and discourse. Theodor Adorno, for example, proclaims that "the essay does not obey the rules of the game of organized science," that it "does not strive for closed, deductive or inductive construction," but instead "proceeds so to speak methodically unmethodically." Thus he asserts that "discontinuity is essential to the essay." In an even more strident expression of this position, William Carlos Williams in "An Essay on Virginia" insists that "unity is the shallowest, the cheapest deception of composition. In nothing is the banality of the intelligence more clearly manifested." And therefore he maintains that genuine "ability in an essay is multiplicity, infinite fracture, the intercrossing of opposed forces establishing any number of opposed centers of stillness." Edward Hoagland does not take so extreme a position as Williams, but "In What I Think, What I Am," he does maintain that "a personal essay is like the human voice talking, its order the mind's natural flow, instead of a systematized outline of ideas." And therefore he observes that it is "more wayward or informal than an article or treatise."

Though I don't consider the essay to be invariably disjointed—it certainly isn't, for example, in the tightly closed narrative pieces of Virginia Woolf, George Orwell, E. B. White, James Baldwin, or Vivian Gornick—I do think that the philosophical significance of discontinuous form has all too often been ignored. Indeed, when segmented form is discussed in handbooks on writing, it is often trivialized as a handy technique borrowed from contemporary journalistic prose. Even someone as thoughtful as Peter Elbow, who devotes an entire chapter to the subject, treats it merely as a convenient "cut and paste" method of writing and revising, a technique for conveying one's ideas implicitly rather than explicitly, a process for getting "rid of everything dead" in one's writing and making something out of one's "good pieces of writing," without having to worry about "trying for coherence and connectedness." Conceived of instead as a mode of embodying the intuitive connections, the complex and often contradictory recollections and reflections of a mind in the process of pondering a particular subject or experience, the discontinuous essay offers a uniquely appropriate form of seriously engaging matters about which one remains profoundly uncertain.

Given the increasing awareness and acceptance of uncertainty or indeterminacy in academic disciplines ranging from nuclear physics to literary theory, discontinuous essays might well be considered a crucial form of reading and writing for students in all fields at all academic levels—a necessary supplement to the more conventionally pointed, methodically structured, and systematically connected discourse that still prevails in most classes. Such tightly closed discourse inevitably encourages students to seek closure and resolution in their perception and conception of any topic under consideration and by extension to favor the kinds of "authoritative" knowledge that will produce definitive conclusions. Discontinuous essays, by contrast, naturally help to develop a healthy tolerance for openness and irresolution in the exploration of material, an awareness and acceptance of the fact that a combination of "various and changeable occurrences," or multiple and shifting perspectives, or personal and academic knowledge, can lead to richly irresolvable complications in one's understanding of a topic, whether it be a season during a troubling time, as in E. B. White's "Spring," or the vexed connections between one's life and one's writing, as in Joyce Carol Oates's "My Father, My Fiction," or a disturbing encounter with a wild animal, as in Annie Dillard's "Living Like Weasels."

––––––––

Several years ago when I was teaching a graduate course in forms of the essay, I lived through a haunting run of experiences, the significance of which still leaves me puzzled. One morning, we were discussing a couple of White's collected essays, "The Geese," a tightly structured narrative piece, and by contrast "The Ring of Time," an embodiment of discontinuous form, looking in detail at the distinct tenor and tempo of each segment in "The Ring of Time." That evening my wife, Kate, and I went to see Woody Allen's "Crimes and Misdemeanors," a movie whose three story lines seemed to me to play off of each other like the parts of a discontinuous essay. Later that evening, I read a piece in *Time* magazine about a new commemorative sculpture designed by Maya Lin, a work whose two differently shaped parts seemed to balance and comment on each other like the plot lines in Allen's movie or the pieces in a discontinuous essay. The next morning Kate and I went out to prune a badly overgrown juniper bush behind our house that almost completely obscured the fifteen-foot-length of a gazebo she had designed, only to discover when we were done that the radiating branches of the juniper and the vertical columns of the gazebo set each other off so well that they seemed to have been as carefully designed for each other as the two parts of Maya Lin's sculpture or as the pieces in White's essay. Before the next class session, I had a few other experiences that seemed related to each other, like the pieces in a discontinuous essay, but exactly how they were connected I could not say for sure. I was then so overwhelmed by the multiplicity, the rapidity, and the mystery of such analogous experiences that it seemed I would have to ponder them at length before I could ever hope to understand them. Perhaps I should have written a discontinuous essay and let the pieces fall where they may.

II Evocations of Personality

VOICES ON VOICE

The Singular "I" and the Chameleon "I"

Voice. You can hear it, can't you? And just think how little it takes to create such an effect. In this case, a one-word opener, a direct address, a question, and an imperative remark—all contributing to the sense of a human presence, of someone talking, giving voice to thought and feeling in an audibly distinctive way. But the voice, of course, is not spoken; it's written. So it's not really audible, except in your mind's ear, unless you happen to be reading it aloud or hear it read aloud by someone else, in which case it's mediated by a distinctly different kind of voice from its own—spoken rather than written. Besides, voice literally refers to a sound so distinctive to each person—a singular combination of pitch, tone, timbre, and inflection—that it could never be reproduced or even approximated in writing. One's voice-print is unique, like one's fingerprint. Still, personal essayists have perennially been so adept at creating the illusion of a spoken voice, a conversational manner, a "familiar style," as Hazlitt calls it, that even when I'm silently reading an essay, I often find myself resonating with something that's hauntingly akin to the sound of a person's voice, as if another person inside my head is talking to me.

The desire of personal essayists to create such an illusion can be traced to Montaigne's persistent espousal of a spontaneous conversational voice. In his essay "On Familiar Style," Hazlitt looks back upon Montaigne as "the first person who in his Essays . . . had the courage to say as an author what he felt as a man. . . . He does not converse with us like a pedagogue to his pupil . . . but like a philosopher and friend." Lamb, in turn, pays special attention to the "uniformly conversational" quality of Hazlitt's essays, which "resemble occasionally the *talk* of a very clever person, when he begins to be animated in a convivial party." High praise from the ventriloquist of Elia. In "The Modern Essay," Virginia Woolf bears witness to such an audible sense of connection that she claims to "look back upon essay after essay by Mr. Beerbohm, knowing that, come September or May, we shall sit down with them and talk," as if to imply that Beerbohm's essays are so animated by a distinctive voice that she could virtually carry on a conversation with them. Edward Hoagland does not go quite so far as Woolf, but he does believe that "a personal essay is like the human voice talking," and that "through its tone and tumbling progression, it conveys the quality of the author's mind."

As these passages suggest, the voice in a personal essay often seems so engaging that it leads one to feel in touch with something animate and sentient beyond the essay—a human presence, or some aspect thereof, that for lack of a better word one may refer to as the essayist, or the mind of the essayist, or the personality of the essayist, or the persona of the essayist. Joyce Carol Oates in *(Woman) Writer* remembers the childhood experience of being so "utterly captivated by another's voice sounding in my ears," that she not only considered such essayists as Emerson and Thoreau to be "voices of adult authenticity" but also came to believe that "the writing attributed to them *was* them." In some sense, of course, the voice in a personal essay does put one in connection with its author, more directly and closely than any other form of writing, except a personal letter. But the nature of that connection is inherently so tangled and indefinite, so variable from one essay or essayist to the next, that despite the strong inclination of some commentators to talk about "authentic voice," one cannot reliably substantiate the connection beyond asserting that it exists. To determine the authenticity of an essayist's voice, one would have to know as much about that essayist's inner life, public behavior, and personal experience as the essayist herself.

Essayists, in fact, rarely claim to achieve an authentic match between their voice and themselves. Instead, they tend to acknowledge some kind of difference and to speak of essayistic personality as involving an element of impersonation or imposture. Montaigne gradually came to recognize the artifice in his seemingly natural voice—"I am quite conscious that sometimes I let myself go too far, and that in the effort to avoid art and affectation, I fall back into them in another direction." E. B. White did not make any pretense about the authenticity of his voice, but claimed in the foreword to his collected essays that "the essayist . . . can pull on any sort of shirt, be any sort of person, according to his mood or his subject matter," admitting as well, "I have worn many shirts, and not all of them have been a good fit." In a similar vein, Nancy Mairs, whose intensely personal essays might seem to be unrehearsed confessions, openly acknowledges in her prelude to *Voice Lessons* that the "I" of her essays is "a construction. I continually make her up as I go along out of whatever materials come to hand." Likewise, Nora Ephron in "Revision and Life," speaks of a time when she wrote innumerable drafts and thereby found "a personal style, a voice if you will, a way of writing that looked chatty and informal."

Voice, according to these essayists, is both an authentic and a fictionalized projection of personality, a resonance that is indisputably related to its author's sense of self but that is also a complex illusion of self. The paradoxical quality of an essayist's voice arises in part out of the natural desire to put on a mask, to impersonate "a character," even (or perhaps, especially) in a personal essay. The irresistible appeal of role-playing is suggested by E. B. White's exuberant listing of the parts an essayist can perform—"philosopher, scold, jester, raconteur, confidant, pundit, devil's advocate, enthusiast." Hoagland bears witness to a similar enthusiasm for role-playing in his assertion that "the artful 'I' of an essay can be as chameleon as any narrator in fiction." Essayistic role-playing has its clearest historical roots in the periodical essayists. But the ultimate source of impersonation probably should be traced to the paradox that exists at the heart of any personal essay, which by virtue of being an act of self-dramatization is at once a masking and an unveiling, a creation and an evocation of self.

Though the connection between voice and self is highly problematic, most discussions of voice tend to suggest otherwise, if only because they invoke such phrases as "having one's own voice," or "having an authentic voice," or "having a distinctive personal voice," or "having the immediacy of a real voice"—phrases that predicate so intimate a connection as to imply that voice is an authentic expression and reflection of self. The grammatically singular form of such expressions also tends to suggest that voice is singular not only in the sense of being distinctive or unique but also in the sense of being a single, unified entity in and of itself. The singular grammatical form of those expressions is, in fact, so deeply ingrained in the idiom that it would be strange indeed, even in a postmodern age, to hear someone speak of an essayist as "having authentic voices," or "having his own voices," or "having distinctive personal voices," though E. B. White's remark about having "worn many shirts" or Edward Hoagland's about "the chameleon" nature of essayists might invite one to think of them as having created such multivoiced selves in their essays. Such remarks might at least suggest that an essayist's voice is likely to change from time to time, as Nancy Mairs makes clear in "Voice Lessons," and as Geoffrey Wolff displays in a lively chronicle of his protean voice, which he describes as having turned from "puffed-up gravitas" to being "increasingly intimate" to being "willing to lighten up, to giggle, to play the fool" to being inspired by the "high-voltage, high-pitched, bully great ruckus" of the sixties to being "less cocksure, I think, more sociable (on the page)."

Despite such confessions, many readers have a natural inclination to perceive each personal essayist as having a distinctive and unchanging voice. Or as Sanders proclaims in "The Singular First Person":

> It is the *singularity* of the first person—its warts and crotchets and turn of voice—that lures many of us into reading essays, and that lingers with us after we finish. Consider the lonely, melancholy persona of Loren Eiseley, forever wandering, forever brooding on our dim and bestial past, his lips frosty with the chill of the Ice Age. Consider the volatile, Dionysian persona of D. H. Lawrence, with his incandescent gaze, his habit of turning peasants into gods and trees into flames, his quick hatred and quicker love. Consider that philosophical farmer Wendell Berry, who speaks with a countryman's knowledge and a deacon's severity. Consider E. B. White, with his cheery affection for brown eggs and dachshunds, his unflappable way of herding geese while the radio warns of an approaching hurricane.

It would be easy to mock such tidy, one-dimensional characterizations—one might even call them caricatures—were I not tempted to focus on such distinctive qualities in my reading of personal essayists. I'm still beguiled, for example, by my own tidy impression of White, as he of the disarmingly modest, wryly humorous voice—ironic rather than cheery—sharing the salty insight born out of his pastoral retreat from the city. I still take pleasure in that voice, still feel its special resonances whenever I turn to his essays, still hear it linger in my ears long after I've finished one of his pieces, even though I've come to realize that the resonance arises from a highly selective perception of White's essays. I hear what I want to hear.

We all hear selectively, of course, picking up some frequencies and tuning out others, particularly given the natural tendency to look for continuities in the works of any author with whom one is familiar. Selective perception, however, is so pronounced in the way we listen to personal essayists that it seems to be the result of a compulsion to dwell on the recurring aspects of an author's voice and thereby invest them with special weight and significance, as Sanders does in his characterizations of Eiseley, Lawrence, Berry, and White. If Sanders is correct, if "the *singularity* of the first person" is what "lures many of us into reading essays" and what "lingers with us after we finish," then it would seem to be the case that our attachment to the personal essay is occasioned in part by a hunger not just for what he refers to as "an idiosyncratic voice in an era of anonymous babble" but also for a stable personality in an unstable time, someone who like Eiseley is "forever brooding," or like Lawrence is forever "volatile," or like Berry is forever "philosophical," or like White is forever "cheery"—though White too often dwells on mortality to be thought of as cheery. Even (or perhaps, especially) in a postmodern age, many readers still hunger for the assurance of being able to find a strong sense of continuity—to hear a distinctively stable voice—throughout the work of any author. And personal essayists can clearly be used to satisfy that hunger, as I and many others have discovered to our satisfaction and self-delusion.

But I have a hunch that such a selective perception of personal essayists may arise not only from an innate hunger to hear continuities of voice but also from so strong an identification with a particular essayist as to obscure the perception of any changes or modulations in that essayist's voice. When I first made the acquaintance of E. B. White's essays, they talked to me, it seemed, in so direct and genial a voice about experiences so akin to my own that I could easily have imagined they were addressed to me and me alone. I too was living near the Maine coast and was learning my way around a sailboat and in turn around its rocky shoreline, as White had some twenty years before. And before my years in Maine, I had lived on a small acreage in upstate New York, where

I tended a little flock of hens and a few ducks, as White had been doing from the time he started living in Maine. So I felt a special kinship with his farming adventures as well as with his saltwater perspective. I too lamented "the shape of television" and the end of passenger service on the Maine railroads. I too had a young son, then only a few years old, whom I wanted to take fishing someday on a lake in Maine.

Given such coincidences, the voice of White's essays resonated for me like an echo of my own experience — an echo that became even more compelling when I discovered that my interest in the craft of prose had its counterpart in his devotion to "the elements of style," even to the extent of doing a textbook on style with Jack Case, the editor who had lured White into updating "the little book." Now, some fifty years later, I'm living in Iowa rather than Maine, I don't sail anymore, don't keep hens anymore, don't worry much about the state of television, and never did take my son to that lake in Maine, though we did get to a reasonable facsimile in Wisconsin. Except for tending a vegetable garden and worrying about the land and the niceties of prose style, my experience nowadays has so little in common with White's that I can see him, I think, more dispassionately and more clearly than before.

My earlier perceptions of his voice began to alter some twenty-five years ago when I had the opportunity to read draft versions of "Dear Mr. 0214 1063 02 10730 08," a satiric piece occasioned by the Federal Reserve ruling of 1967 that instituted the nationwide use of computer-coded checks. In the first of his handwritten notes for that essay, I heard a ponderous, solemn, and preachy voice that I hadn't remembered him using before, not even in his most serious pieces on controversial public issues: "The danger in a machine culture is that in the enjoyment of the convenience of machines, we will overshadow their disadvantages to others." And he wasn't any more adept in his second version of the idea: "The danger in a machine culture is that the convenience of machines may come to overshadow the losses we suffer by reason of their peculiar arrangements." Where, I wondered, was the deft touch I'd come to associate with White? Had "the danger in a machine culture" caused him to lose control of his voice — of his knack for conveying an idea in a crisp image or witty turn of phrase? White evidently noticed the laboriousness of those passages, for neither one appeared in his first typewritten draft, a more playful piece than anything in his notes.

Nothing even hinting at the "danger in a machine culture" or "the losses we suffer from them" appeared in the first typewritten draft, as if to suggest that White could reclaim the witty voice of his essays only by making fun of the Federal Reserve, of computer-legible numbers, of his local bank, and of himself—in other words, by completely avoiding the serious implications of his topic. But those implications nagged at him enough that he brought them back into his second typewritten draft, though in a much more deft style and wryly humorous voice:

> I'm not against machines, as are some people who feel that the computer is leading us down the primrose trail. I like machines—particularly the egg-beater, which is the machine at its finest and most mysterious. I'm only against machines when the convenience they afford to some overshadows the inconvenience they cause to all.

Having found a playful but pointed way to register his concern with the "danger" of machines, White revised the passage yet again to produce a final version that is even more emphatic and stylistically well turned:

> I'm not against machines, as are some people who feel the computer is leading us back into the jungle. I rather like machines, particularly the egg-beater, which is the highest point the machine has yet reached. I'm against machines only when the convenience they afford to some people is regarded as more important than the inconvenience they cause to all.

Reviewing the different formulations of that idea in his notes and typewritten drafts, I was struck by the numerous changes that White had made to achieve his customarily plain wording and carefully structured phrasing. Four separate drafts, as well as interlinear revisions, for a 750 word essay! But I was most impressed by how those stylistic revisions had turned the solemn and directly voiced concern of his notes into the ironic, playful, and complexly voiced stance of his final draft. Such a drastic alteration that it made me realize the craftiness of that engaging voice I'd always considered to be an uncontrived reflection of White. Such a striking alteration that it also made me realize he had more voices than one, and that each voice, no matter how different from the other, must have reflected some aspect of himself, if only because they both existed in writing. Given that the solemn one was confined largely to his notes, I thought of it as the expression of an inner self, reflecting the concern that White must have felt when he first heard of the Federal Reserve's decree. But since White did not choose to develop that voice in subsequent versions of the essay, it also seemed reasonable to assume that he looked upon it as a private voice, to be replaced largely, but not completely, by the more familiar public voice of his essays. An echo of his solemn and earnest voice could still be heard in the assertion that "I'm against machines only when the convenience they afford to some people is regarded as more important than the inconvenience they cause to all." But the earnestness had been so diminished by the context as well as by the revised wording that it seemed almost inaudible—almost completely hidden.

Though I'd not sensed any pretense in White's essays prior to reading the draft versions of "Dear Mr. 0214 1063 02 10730 08," I had recently read the "Foreword" to his collected essays, in which he exuberantly depicted the essayist as a chameleon-like actor, who "can pull on any sort of shirt, be any sort of person, according to his mood or subject matter." When I first encountered that passage, I didn't quite understand how it could apply to White and his essays. Though his "mood" certainly changed both from essay to essay and within a single piece, it didn't seem that he changed "his garb" or that he changed into a different "sort of person." His voice had always seemed to be so stable from one essay to the next that he appeared to be the same "sort of person" from one essay to the next. As constant and unchanging as that favorite lake of his in Maine. But after reading that passage in the context of what he said in a letter to Margo Todd about writing as "a form of imposture" and of what I had heard in the several versions of "Dear Mr. 0214 1063 02 10730 08," I thought there might be more voices, more poses, in his essays than I had imagined, though I didn't know what to make of that supposition back then.

My inquiries remained at a standstill for several years, until I was rereading "Once More to the Lake," "The Ring of Time," and "The Geese" for an essay I planned to write about White's preoccupation with time, change, and mortality. Though I'd read those essays several times, I didn't remember any significant differences in his voice from one to the next, except of course for tonal differences occasioned by differences in his mood or subject matter, such as the reverie in his early memories of the lake, the admiration in his description of the young circus rider, and the sorrow in his account of the defeated old gander. But this time, reading the essays in conjunction with each other, I noticed substantial differences in his voice—differences that dramatically outweighed any similarities in the plainness of his language or the straightforwardness of his phrasing. The differences were so clear-cut that I could hear them at the start of each piece:

> One summer, along about 1904, my father rented a camp on a lake in Maine and took us all there for the month of August. We all got ringworm from some kittens and had to rub Pond's extract on our arms and legs night and morning, and my father rolled over in a canoe with all his clothes on; but outside of that the vacation was a success and from then on none of us ever thought there was any place in the world like that lake in Maine.

> After the lions had returned to their cages, creeping angrily through the chutes, a little bunch of us drifted away and into an open doorway nearby, where we stood for a while in semidarkness, watching a big grown circus horse go harumphing around the practice ring. His trainer was a woman of about forty, and the two of them, horse and woman, seemed caught up in one of those desultory treadmills of afternoon from which there is no apparent escape.

> To give a clear account of what took place in the barnyard early in the morning on that last Sunday in June, I will have to go back more than a year in time, but a year is nothing to me these days. Besides, I intend to be quick about it and not dawdle.

Reading each of those passages, I was struck by how different a voice, how different a personality, he was able to project in just the space of two sentences. In the opening of "Once More to the Lake," for example, I heard the voice of a child, particularly in the second sentence, with its youthful idiom and its incessant compounding of clauses and verb phrases, suggestive of an enthusiastic young boy in the heady rush of remembering. In "The Ring of Time," by contrast, I heard him speaking at the start in the much more deliberate voice of someone mature enough and jaded enough to know about "those desultory treadmills of afternoon from which there is no apparent escape," also someone sophisticated enough with language to convey such an adult view of things in a complexly varied pair of sentences. At the opening of "The Geese," by contrast with each of the others, I heard a somewhat stiff, old-fashioned style and rural idiom suggestive of a self-important, plain-talking farmer, preoccupied as much with his age as with his harvest. Hearing such different voices, I realized for the first time that White was, indeed, a chameleon—that he cast himself as "a different sort of person" in each of those essays.

Those three essays, in turn, led me to perceive his impersonations as being far more elaborate than even he had intimated in his remarks on the essayist's poses. For in none of the three did he stick to his opening voice. In "Once More to the Lake," just a couple of sentences after his childlike opening voice, I heard the intonations of a much more mature consciousness, reflected in the gist of his remarks, the elevation of his language, and the sophistication of his syntax:

> I have since become a salt-water man, but sometimes in
> summer there are days when the restlessness of the tides and
> the fearful cold of the sea water and the incessant wind that
> blows across the afternoon and into the evening make me wish
> for the placidity of a lake in the woods.

During most of the essay, he maintained that mature voice, except for several moments when he clearly moved back into a boyish style and idiom, piling up the recollections as he had at the beginning. And at one point, midway through the essay, I heard a strikingly different presence, resonating with the ecstatic apostrophe of a nineteenth-century poet:

> Summertime, oh, summertime, pattern of life indelible, the
> fadeproof lake, the woods unshatterable, the pasture with the
> sweetfern, forever and ever, summer without end.

Hearing the interplay of those different voices, I came to feel that White must have intended them as a means of enacting the complex psychic experience he had gone through during his return to the lake. For the alternating voices of the boy and man clearly paralleled the "creepy sensation" he had repeatedly experienced of perceiving his son as his childhood self and himself as his own father— confusions of identity reflecting the coexistence within him of two distinctly different selves. The exultant, celebratory voice, invoking "summer without end," just as clearly seemed to embody the illusion that animated both boy and man. Hearing the dramatic interplay of those voices, I also came to understand why the ending of the essay had always moved me so strongly, for in the syntactically controlled resonances of his concluding voice I could virtually feel White's middle-aged self definitively resolving the confusion and dispelling the illusion that had beguiled him up to that point:

> Languidly, and with no thought of going in, I watched him, his hard little body, skinny and bare, saw him wince slightly as he pulled up around his vitals the small, soggy, icy garment. As he buckled the belt, suddenly my groin felt the chill of death.

If the multivoiced quality of "Once More to the Lake" were unique or unusual among White's essays, I'd have been less inclined to discuss it here in such detail. But the prevalence of this quality is unmistakable in many of his pieces. In the two parts of "The Ring of Time," White sustains an even more complex array of voices and postures. In the first part, centered on the enchanting spectacle of a young circus girl riding her horse around the practice ring, White gradually emerges from the somewhat jaded voice he had assumed at the beginning of the piece and becomes a role-playing acrobat himself, first stepping forward in a playfully self-regarding comment on his status as "recording secretary for one of the oldest societies—the society of those who, at one time or another, have surrendered, without even a show of resistance to the bedazzlement of a circus rider." Then just a bit later, he turns from being the playfully confessional enthusiast of the circus to speaking in the voice of a much more thoughtful, even philosophical observer, when the young circus rider makes him "painfully conscious," as he puts it, "of the element of time." Then just a few paragraphs later, he reclaims the voice of a playfully self-regarding commentator, this time on his supposedly failed acrobatics as a writer. Each of these voices and guises is occasioned by his shifting thoughts about the circus rider's performance, about his own performance, and about the ring of time.

In yet another display of his protean behavior, White speaks in a somewhat different set of voices during the second segment of "The Ring of Time," as he tries not only to evoke the rhythm of life and the movement of time in the South but also to reflect upon racial problems in the segregated South of the 1950s. At the beginning of the second segment, he appears in the guise of a verbal musician, playing a riff upon the letter "s": "Everywhere, for the appreciative visitor, the letter 's' insinuates itself in the scene: in the sound of sea and sand, in the singing shell, in the heat of sun and sky, in the sultriness of the gentle hours, in the siesta, in the stir of birds and insects." A couple of pages later, however, reflecting on the southern resistance to racial integration, he assumes the voice of a deft social critic: "Probably the first slave ship, with Negroes lying in chains on its decks, seemed commonsensical to the owners who operated it and to the planters who patronized it. But such a vessel would not be in the realm of common sense today." And then just a couple of paragraphs later, the voice of the social critic gives way to the stance of the vacationer: "Lying in the warm comfort by the sea, you receive gratefully the gift of the sun, the gift of the South."

Confronted by such a striking array of voices and poses both in "The Ring of Time" and in "The Geese"—where White speaks not only in the voice of the crusty barnyard detective, but also in the voices of an overly fretful farmer, a witty raconteur, and a compassionate old man—one might be moved to wonder if there is any element of consistency in White's essayistic self, or if he assumes so many different voices and postures as to have no abiding and distinctive voice at all. At first thought, it's tempting to note that despite the wide range of different voices, there's also a recurrent voice that tends to prevail or at least to have the last word in many of those essays, such as the voice of the mature man who holds forth in "Once More to the Lake," or the discerning social critic who emerges in the second segment of "The Ring of Time," or the compassionate barnyard observer who laments the fate of the old gander at the end of "The Geese." But in each case, these serious voices often alternate with playful or wryly humorous sides of White's essayistic personality that it would be misleading to ignore. In fact, White traverses a wide tonal or attitudinal range in many of his essays, and not just from one essay to the next but often from one segment or paragraph of an essay to the next. Given his tendency to move quickly and deftly from the nostalgic to the buoyant, the reflective to the playful, the sardonic to the comic, and back again, it seems difficult to pin him down, especially when one recognizes that he tends to dramatize those different states of mind and feeling by embodying them in different voices. His voice encompasses such a wide range of voices that perhaps it would be most accurate to talk about the voice(s), or the multivoiced personality, of E. B. White.

Against such a view, it might be argued that White's voice is ultimately determined by the plain wording, the careful phrasing, the meticulously and vividly detailed description to be found in most of his essays. His style, one might say, is completely in keeping with the rules laid down in Strunk and White — rules that have the effect of producing a candid and unpretentious voice, the voice of someone whose statements can be taken at face value. But those stylistic traits, no matter how distinctive they seem to be, do not constitute the sole source of White's voice, as one can see by looking at the following piece of description:

> Before the swallow, before the daffodil, and not much later than the snowdrop, the common toad salutes the coming of spring after his own fashion, which is to emerge from a hole in the ground, where he has lain buried since the previous autumn, and crawl as rapidly as possible toward the nearest suitable patch of water.

This piece of natural observation has all the characteristic marks of White's prose style: the plain and simple words, mostly one or two syllables long as in the opening of "Once More to the Lake"; the parallel phrasing of coordinate ideas as stipulated in Strunk and White; the vividly detailed and well-informed description of the toad's behavior; and the witty but understated personification of the toad who "salutes the coming of spring after his own fashion." But as it happens, this sentence and others exactly like it come from the opening of an essay by George Orwell, "Some Thoughts on the Common Toad." Though style is a significant determinant of voice, it's evidently not the sole determinant. Equally important is the character of the human presence that one creates out of any particular style, and in this particular passage Orwell is typically self-effacing rather than "congenitally self-centered," as White exuberantly professes to be. Orwell's attention is focused entirely on the toad without any mention of himself, and thus the passage lacks the presence of White observing the toad that I would expect to find in one of his essays.

Though White's protean behavior may seem unusual or extreme, it represents a quality that is evident, though perhaps to a somewhat lesser degree, in many personal essayists. Lamb and Hazlitt come immediately to mind, as do Beerbohm and more recently Edward Hoagland, Nancy Mairs, Alice Walker, and Philip Lopate. Most human beings, after all, perform a variety of roles during just a single day in their lives, as they move back and forth between public and private situations, so it's hardly surprising that an essayist, as White says, "can pull on any sort of shirt, be any sort of person, according to his mood or subject matter." One might even claim that the capacity and willingness to do so are essential to the creation of authentically personal essays—essays, that is, in which a personality comes to life in something like the rich variety of its actual being. The drama of one's personality depends, after all, on the *dramatis personae* one is capable of performing. I don't mean to imply that every personal essayist is, or need be, multivoiced. But I do believe that the myth of a singular and unchanging voice has tended to distort the perception and understanding of personal essays and essayists. And it may also have subverted instruction in the writing of personal essays. How many teachers of writing, I wonder, invite their students to produce essays in which they play a variety of roles, put on a variety of shirts, speak in a variety of voices? How many even invite their students to try out different voices in different essays? How many invite them to write personal essays that are true to the range and richness of their actual voices?

The myth of "finding one's voice" strongly implies that once having found it, one will never lose it, never change it. But the nature of experience suggests otherwise, as Montaigne makes clear in his Heraclitean assertion that "I may presently change, not only by chance, but also by intention," and as Didion affirms when she declares that "keeping a notebook" is a way "to keep in touch with the people we used to be, whether we find them attractive company or not." So, perhaps the changing voices I've noted in White's three essays may be the result of his having written them fifteen years apart—"Once More to the Lake" in 1940, when he was forty-one, "The Ring of Time" in 1955, when he was fifty-six, and "The Geese" in 1970, when he was seventy-one. The voice of a personal essayist may, after all, be as mutable as life itself.

Walking into Tio Pepe's, I never imagined that dining there in Baltimore, amid the lamp-lit stucco walls of a Spanish restaurant, bristling with red-jacketed waiters and bullfighting scenes, would lead to this piece on Elia, the pseudonymous self of Charles Lamb. Oh yes, I went there intending to dine on roast suckling pig, a specialty of the chef and subject of Elia's renowned "Dissertation," so one might say I was tacitly committed to doing the kind of primary research that could lead to an essay such as this. But I would hasten to reply that my hunger for the suckling was roused not by an interest in Elia but by somewhat different motives, for I was eager to determine whether the roasted creature warranted so flamboyant a tribute as Lamb's that I too might be moved to such essayistic effusions. After all, I had traveled to Baltimore to serve as visiting essayist at a local university, and how better to fulfill that role than to walk in the footsteps of such an illustrious predecessor—he might even have savored his roast pig in a Georgian building like the nineteenth-century brick edifice that houses Tio Pepe's. So if truth be known, I had in mind a literary communion of sorts, a partaking of flesh akin to "the crisp, tawny, well-watched, not over-roasted, crackling" that had moved Elia to proclaim "of all the delicacies in the whole *mundus edibilis*, I will maintain it to be the most delicate—*princeps obsoniorum*."

Not having sampled the entire world of delicacies, I was hardly in a position to declare the suckling pig I dined on that night, the Conchinillo Asado Estilo Segovia, to be the most distinguished of all meats. But it sure was a mouthful. Such exquisite crackling, such tender flesh, "such animal manna"—the very first taste of it made me feel I had never understood "A Dissertation upon Roast Pig," because I had never had a gustatory experience sufficient to illuminate the source of its inspiration. I, who had taught it on numerous occasions throughout my academic career, guiding students through its five-part structure (culinary history, epideictic oratory, personal reminiscence, ethical inquiry, pithy recipe), each part with its own distinctive style, as if the whole were an elaborate jeu d'esprit—I, who might have written a dissertation upon Elia's dissertation, suddenly realized, as never before, that Lamb's game was deadly earnest. More earnest, by far, than I had ever imagined. Who, after all, having dined on roast suckling pig could fail to be enthralled by its incomparable flavor and texture, by the striking contrast between its buttery flesh and ineffable crackling? And who having tasted such a supreme dish could write about it without succumbing to hyperbole? Or so I thought in that first moment of ingestion. Yet Lamb sustained a playfully exaggerated style without becoming so extravagant as to mock the impulse that engendered such hyperbole or render himself a fit subject for mockery. A delicate balance indeed.

With each precious morsel—bathed, it should be noted, in a sensuous gravy—I found myself pondering Elia's dissertation and Elia himself not only with greater admiration but also with a heightened sense of curiosity, wondering what more I might discover by revisiting the dissertation, savoring it once again as I had never done before. But no sooner did I vow to renew my acquaintance with Lamb's performance therein than it occurred to me that perhaps I could not fully appreciate Elia's behavior in that excursion without taking note of his conduct in other essays published under that fictitious name. So it was that Tio Pepe's Conchinillo Asado led me back to the essays of Elia and anything else that might shed light on that remarkable personage.

———

Elia made his debut without any editorial fanfare in the *London Magazine* of August 1820, in such a strange and haunting essay, "The South Sea House," that readers were evidently fascinated as much by him as by the piece itself. And with good reason. What an eccentric he must have seemed to be obsessed with the decaying headquarters and skeleton staff of such a diminished enterprise as the South Sea Company, justifying his focus on them with a starkly simple closing assertion—"Their importance is from the past." A nostalgist par excellence. How quirky also to write about the company not as it had been one hundred years earlier, during the notorious South Sea bubble, but as it existed in 1780, at a time of no particular importance (eleven years before Lamb himself was briefly employed there). And how strange he must have sounded, buttonholing his readers at the beginning of the piece with a direct address, then luring them into the grammatical intricacies of a periodic sentence (periodic question, to be exact) with an intriguing parenthetical reference to himself, the supposed author of the piece, "a lean annuitant" (residing ironically in a very expansive sentence):

> READER, in thy passage from the Bank—where thou hast been receiving thy half-yearly dividends (supposing thou art a lean annuitant like myself)—to the Flower Pot, to secure a place of Dalston or Shacklewell, or some other thy suburban retreat northerly,—didst thou never observe a melancholy looking, handsome, brick and stone edifice, to the left— where Threadneedle-street abuts upon Bishopsgate?

Here was an unusual presence, indeed—so roundabout compared to the straightforward manner of others in the magazine that readers might well have been struck by his antiquated style and his breathless description of the South Sea House in a sentence that runs on for almost two hundred words, piling phrase upon phrase in a welter of accumulating images:

> stately porticos; imposing staircases; offices roomy as the state apartments in palaces—deserted or thinly peopled with a few straggling clerks; the still more sacred interiors of court and committee rooms, with venerable faces of beadles, door keepers—directors seated in form on solemn days (to proclaim a dead dividend) at long worm-eaten tables, that have been mahogany, with tarnished gilt-leather coverings, supporting massy silver inkstands long since dry.

A vivid account of decayed grandeur, Elia's detailed tour of the building served as a striking prelude to portraits of the South Sea clerks themselves—each so pointedly delineated as to reflect a discerning observer, each so expressively worded as to suggest an intense personal involvement, undiminished by the passage of time: "Can I forget thee Henry Man, the wit, the polished man of letters, the *author*, of the South Sea House? who never enteredst thy office in a morning, or quittedst it in mid-day—(what didst *thou* in thy office?)—without some quirk that left a sting!" Given such a double-edged habit of mind, often turning from affectionate to biting recollection in the space of a sentence or parenthesis, readers of "The South Sea House" might well have been at once fascinated and puzzled by his contradictory reactions. And their bafflement would not have been allayed by Elia's whimsically concluding remarks about the veracity of his piece: "Reader, what if I have been playing with thee all the while—peradventure the very *names*, which I have summoned up before thee, are fantastic—insubstantial. . . . Be satisfied that something answering to them has had a being. Their importance is from the past."

Far from being fantastic, the names that Elia had summoned up corresponded to South Sea clerks whom Lamb observed when he was briefly employed there in 1791 (eleven years after the time referred to in the essay), as Lamb made clear in a letter (July 30, 1821) to John Taylor, his editor at the *London Magazine*. But the eleven-year gap suggests that Lamb had also been "playing with" his readers "all the while," as suggested by a letter (August 16, 1820) to his longtime friend Barron Field, shortly before "The South Sea House" was published, in which he spoke of it as "a tissue of truth and fiction impossible to be extricated." The quintessential embodiment of that paradoxical weave was Elia himself—anagram for "a lie," as one of Lamb's friends reportedly claimed. Anagram or not, most readers of the period would have regarded that single name at the end of the essay as a singularly indecipherable pseudonym, distinctly different from such tag-like pen names as the Tatler, the Spectator, and the Rambler, as well as from pseudonyms based on classical Greek and Roman names, such as Crito, Edax, and Pensilis, which Lamb had used for some of his earlier periodical essays. Enigmatic though it was, the source of Elia's name lay closer at hand than most of his readers could have realized, for according to Lamb it was the name of an Italian clerk who had worked at the South Sea House during his brief time there but who died a year before "The South Sea House" appeared in print. Thus in using the name of Elia, Lamb appropriated the identity of someone with a firsthand knowledge of the South Sea House, but in taking the name of a dead man, it might also be said that Lamb had engaged in identity theft, though he claimed to have used it rather than his own in consideration of his brother John, who held the title of accountant at the

South Sea House and might not have enjoyed some of his disparaging descriptions.

Whatever Lamb's initial motives for that eccentric pseudonym and style, he could hardly ignore the curiosity aroused by Elia, teasingly acknowledging it two months later in the opening of his next essay, "Oxford in the Vacation"—"methinks I hear you exclaim, Reader, *Who is Elia?*" But he withheld that simple question until the end of yet another elaborately suspended sentence, this one featuring a witty parenthetical observation within an extended analogy, so deftly spun out that Elia's intricate prose might well have been regarded as the hallmark of his identity:

> CASTING a preparatory glance at the bottom of this article — as the wary connoisseur in prints, with cursory eye (which, while it reads, seems as though it read not,) never fails to consult the quis sculpsit in the corner, before he pronounces some rare piece to be a Vivares, or a Woolet—methinks I hear you exclaim, Reader, Who is Elia?

Elia, of course, avoided a direct answer to the question but in a roundabout manner did finally "agnize" himself to be a "votary of the desk," spending the "forepart" of his days with "figures and cyphers," and the latter part amid "the flowery carpet-ground of a midnight dissertation." A pattern so akin to Lamb's daily life and so much of a piece with other parallels between Elia and Lamb—in bookish interests and literary ventures—that it's tempting to regard Elia as synonymous with Lamb, except for a few minor differences. Indeed, a few paragraphs later in the same essay, Elia alludes to the time when he "was at school at Christ's," much as Lamb had been, and a bit later on speaks of having been "defrauded in his young years of the sweet food of academic institution," much as Lamb's stuttering deprived him of a chance for admission to a university.

The parallels are so numerous it's not surprising that many commentators have been inclined to regard Elia as merely a pseudonym for Lamb. An equation given greater credence by Lamb's postmortem portrait of Elia, "A Character of the Late Elia" (January 1823), which sometimes reads like a wry self-portrait, particularly given its detailed attention to such telling details as Elia's stutter, his provocative social behavior, the character of his friends, and his work at the East India House. Thus in years past, I too was inclined toward such an equation, but not since comparing Lamb's correspondence, critical essays, and reviews, to the Elia essays both as they first appeared in the *London Magazine* and in collected form. Now, on the contrary, I'm inclined to see Elia as an alternative self —a pseudonym endowed with a distinctive persona and style so different from Lamb's other nonfiction as to constitute a pseudonymous self extraordinaire unique in the history of the personal essay.

Pseudonyms are such a conventional and superficial form of disguise in the eighteenth- and early-nineteenth-century periodical essay that they might well be considered an inconsequential gesture, especially when the pseudonymous self, such as Johnson's Rambler, is indistinguishable in style and outlook from the self embodied in the rest of an author's prose. But that is hardly true of Elia, whose antiquated style, nostalgic temperament, and irrepressible whimsy dramatically set him apart from the no-nonsense voice of Lamb's reviews and other nonfiction pieces, as well as the more intimate and chatty persona of his letters. Lamb was acutely aware of the difference and took pains to prevent himself from being equated with Elia. Indeed, the first collection of Elia essays, published in 1823, was entitled *Elia: Essays Published Under that Signature in the London Magazine*, without any mention of Lamb's name either on the title page or anywhere else in the volume. A notable instance of authorial self-effacement. And in December 1825, Lamb wrote a brief letter to Charles Ollier, a subeditor of the *New Monthly*, asserting that his columns for that magazine "had better have L. signd to them and reserve *Elia* for Essays more *Eliacal*." Thus Lamb thought of Elia as having such a different style and temperament from his other nonfiction writing that he sought to preserve the distinction not only by using different signatures for each but also by inventing an adjective, "Eliacal," to highlight the difference. Lamb's insistence on the difference suggests that in writing the essays of Elia, he considered himself to be impersonating someone other than himself. By September 1825, in fact, he had evidently exhausted his interest in the role, and from then until his death in 1834, he wrote no more pieces under the pseudonym of Elia.

Lamb's decision to impersonate a nostalgic and whimsical character had its roots no doubt in a prior attraction to the past, manifest in his "Recollections of Christ's Hospital," a memory piece that he wrote in 1813. But his creation of Elia was also motivated by a critical overview of the essay that he evidently developed during the intervening years and that led him to regard a distinctive persona as fundamental to an essayist's success. A sine qua non, as Lamb made clear at the start of an unpublished review of Hazlitt's *Table Talk* that he wrote just two or three months before Elia's first appearance in "The South Sea House":

> A series of Miscellaneous Essays, however well executed in the parts, if it have not some pervading character to give a unity to it, is ordinarily as tormenting to get through as a set of aphorisms, or a jest-book. The fathers of Essay writing in ancient and modern times — Plutarch in a measure, and Montaigne without mercy or measure — imparted their own personal peculiarities to their themes. By this balm are they preserved. The author of the Rambler in a less direct way has attained the same effect.

By contrast with his praise for the "personal peculiarities" of Plutarch, Montaigne, and Johnson, Lamb took the Spectator to task because "he writes finely upon all subjects — but himself. He sets every thing in a proper light — but we do not see through his spectacles. He colours nothing with his own hues." Having established such a pointed historical contrast, Lamb celebrated Hazlitt for being "of the class of Essayists first mentioned. He attracts, or repels, by strong realities of individual observation, humour, and feeling." He not only affirmed Hazlitt's singular persona but also paid special attention to its deliberateness: "The Writer almost every where adopts the style of a discontented man. This assumption of a character, if it be not truly (as we are inclined to believe) his own, is that which gives force & life to his writing." Hazlitt's deliberate manner, together with the precedents of Plutarch, Montaigne, and Johnson, evidently inspired Lamb to assume an equally striking persona by adopting the antiquarian style and temperament of a nostalgic and whimsical man. Or as he said in his mock epitaph for Elia, "My late friend was in many respects a singular character."

Lamb had an even more compelling reason for his sustained impersonation of Elia, a personal motive that can best be described as a veiled autobiographical intent, reflected in the numerous memory pieces that focus on persons, places, and episodes in Elia's "life" which correspond to aspects of Lamb's past—names, dates, and other details having been altered, as in a roman à clef. Lamb not only renamed his brother John and his sister Mary (James and Bridget) but also turned them from siblings into cousins in "My Relations"; likewise, he renamed his father Lovel in "The Old Benchers of the Inner Temple" and did not even identify him as Elia's father or relative of any kind. A by-product, no doubt, of Lamb's intent to remain in the background. Reticent though he was, Lamb's desire to tell his story was irrepressible, which led him to adapt and incorporate material from his personal experience, inventing or borrowing additional characters and incidents as need be. But Elia's memories so often put a good face on things that collectively they suggest a wished-for life rather than the one that Lamb endured. He made no reference whatsoever to his sister's crazed murder of their mother, nor to his sister's manic-depressive attacks—indeed, he only hints at her eccentricity in "Mackery End, in Hertfordshire," as if their lives together were as buoyant and genial as their latter day visit to Mackery End. And no mention of his own bouts of melancholia until "The Convalescent" (July 1825), the penultimate Elia essay, occasioned by a profound period of depression that Lamb experienced following his retirement from the East India House. Given so many omissions and fictional alterations, it's hardly surprising that in a footnote to "The Old Benchers of the Inner Temple," which appeared in the magazine but not in the collected version, Elia speaks of his "narratives" as "shadows of fact—verisimilitudes, not verities—or sitting but upon the remote edges and outskirts of history."

Lamb used Elia not just to produce a rose-colored autobiography in disguise. He also used him to speak out on a wide range of subjects—from modes of thought to styles of acting, from card games to chimney sweeps, from the abuse of women to the preparation of roast pig. In this respect, one might say that Elia was both an alternative self and a mouthpiece, bearing witness to thoughts and convictions that were sometimes more daring than might be expected of the whimsical reminiscer who appeared in "The South Sea House" and elsewhere. Elia first shocked readers in "New Year's Eve" (January 1821) with his refusal to find comfort in the idea of an afterlife:

I am not content to pass away "like a weaver's shuttle." Those metaphors solace me not, nor sweeten the unpalatable draught of mortality. I care not to be carried with the tide, that smoothly bears human life to eternity; and reluct at the inevitable course of destiny. I am in love with this green earth; the face of town and country; the unspeakable rural solitudes, and the sweet security of streets. I would set up my tabernacle here.

Can a ghost laugh, or shake his sides, when you are pleasant with him?

Given such devout thoughts about life and such scornful ones about an afterlife, it's not surprising that Elia offended the religious sensibilities of nineteenth-century readers. Thomas Southey accused him of lacking "a sounder religious feeling," and a long poetical "Epistle to Elia," signed "Olen," urged him to consider the sure rewards of a Christian faith as well as the cherished friends and relatives he would meet in heaven. But in a letter to his editor (July 30, 1821), Elia's skepticism was unyielding: "Poor Elia . . . does not pretend to so very clear revelations of a future state of being as 'Olen' seems gifted with." He was even more contrary in "Modern Gallantry" (September 1821), a piece exposing the sham of "deferential respect, which we are supposed to pay to females as females." In a climactically arranged series of parallel statements, as in an oration rather than an essay, Elia stridently enunciated the abuses of women that then prevailed—so fierce in his attack that he should be considered an early feminist:

> I shall believe that this principle actuates our conduct, when I can forget, that in the nineteenth century of the era from which we date our civility, we are but just beginning to leave off the very frequent practice of whipping females in public, in common with the coarsest male offenders.
>
> I shall begin to believe that there is some such principle influencing our conduct, when more than one-half of the drudgery and coarse servitude of the world shall cease to be performed by women.

In the face of such heightened rhetoric, one might be moved to ask how the nostalgist of "The South Sea House" or the bibliophile of "Oxford in the Vacation" could plausibly morph into the religious skeptic of "New Year's Eve" or the social reformer of "Modern Gallantry." But those personae and their attitudes are not mutually exclusive. Besides, Elia's sharply critical eye is manifest both in "The South Sea House" and "Oxford in the Vacation," much as his nostalgic inclinations and human sympathies are evident in "New Year's Eve" and "Modern Gallantry." Such continuities, however, should not obscure the fact that Elia is a protean character, "making himself many, or reducing many unto himself," as Lamb made clear in his epitaph for Elia. Indeed, judging from the essays themselves, Lamb was capable of imagining and enacting a wide array of postures within the role of Elia, even to the extent of reversing himself and playing a part directly at odds with his prior attitudes and experience. In "Christ's Hospital Five and Thirty Years Ago," for example, Lamb crafted a surprise opening for Elia by having him take "Mr. Lamb" to task for writing an imbalanced celebration of the school in a previously published essay, "Recollections of Christ's Hospital" (1813). Writing as if from the viewpoint of someone whose parents and friends "were far away" from the school, like his lonely schoolmate Coleridge, Lamb not only presented a critical view of the school for the unfair advantages that it offered to students who lived in London as he did, but also projected a clear-cut difference between himself and Elia, thereby endowing Elia with the authenticity of a person in his own right and a background distinct from Lamb's:

> I remember L. at school; and can well recollect that he had
> some advantages, which I and others of his schoolfellow had
> not. His friends lived in town, and were near at hand; and he
> had the privilege of going to see them, almost as often as he
> wished, through some invidious distinction, which was denied
> to us.

And it should be noted that in this instance, Lamb endowed Elia with a remarkably straightforward and plainly worded style, the complete antithesis of his previously "antique modes and phrases."

Lamb was so intent on portraying Elia as a many-sided, multivoiced personage that he sometimes penned combative letters by Elia that appeared in the correspondence section of the *London Magazine*, in response to critical notes about Elia that the magazine had previously published. In the November 1821 issue, he referred to one correspondent as "a tinkling cymbal" and dismissed his critique as "obvious rhodomontade." And when his good friend and fellow essayist Leigh Hunt reprinted a celebratory review of Lamb's work, with a prefatory note briefly mentioning that he occasionally writes "under the signature of Elia," Lamb sought to counter the revelation by producing a lengthy "P.S." to "A Chapter on Ears" (March 1821), in which Elia makes a defense of his authorship and actuality that is alternately witty, passionate, and morally outraged. The "P.S.," which appeared in the *London Magazine* but not in *Elia*, begins with a tongue-in-cheek reference to Hunt as an "assumed signature" for "a writer, whose real name, it seems, is *Boldero*"—a tit for tat, as it were—playfully turning the accusation back upon Hunt. But Elia's jesting mood soon gives way to self-pity about the timing of Hunt's assertion, "affording no scope for explanation for a full month—during which time, I must needs lie writhing and tossing, under the cruel imputation of nonentity." Such a melodramatic exaggeration that it seems like a playful hyperbole. Then Elia's distress abruptly turns into a rhetorically fierce expression of outrage:

> They call this an age of personality: but surely this spirit of anti-personality (if I may presume to express it) is something worse.
> Take away my moral reputation: I may live to discredit that calumny.
> Injure my literary fame,—I may write that up again—
> But when a gentleman is robbed of his identity, where is he?
> Other murderers stab but at our existence, a frail and perishing trifle at the best. But here is an assassin who aims at our very essence; who not only forbids us *to be* any longer, but *to have been* at all.

Elia's anger continues to build through another lengthy paragraph, reaching the heightened emotional climax of a bravura performance—"I am ashamed that this trifling writer should have power to move me so." A daring conclusion, given the long-standing friendship between Lamb and Hunt, a friendship that evidently continued despite this piece, judging from Lamb's correspondence.

Elia's rage at being "robbed of his identity" is, of course, ironic, given the numerous styles and stances of which he is made. A passel of poses, created by an impresario, he constitutes a supremely artful challenge to the idea of "personality" that he passionately invokes. For nostalgic and whimsical though Elia is, at least to begin with and intermittently thereafter, he displays so many other qualities that it would not be an exaggeration to say he is polymorphous — shape-shifting and style-switching from one piece to the next. Sometimes "an affected array of antique modes and phrases," as in "The South Sea House" and "Oxford in the Vacation," but sometimes straight-forwardly plain and mournful, as in "Dream Children: A Reverie," sometimes rhetorically fierce and up-to-date, as in "Modern Gallantry," sometimes playfully self-absorbed, as in "A Chapter on Ears," sometimes free-thinking and contrary, as in "Grace before Meat." So many different postures, in fact, that it seems as if Lamb was not content to impersonate a "pervading character," such as he initially envisioned, but chose instead to role-play a protean figure, while also sustaining an illusion of unity amid the shifting masks and personae. In crafting such a literary tour-de-force as Elia, Lamb tacitly raised questions about the very nature of personality, as if to suggest that it might, at last, be as fluid and fabricated a thing as language itself. And Lamb, therefore, as much a postmodernist as a romantic.

Viewed in this context, "A Dissertation upon Roast Pig" is surely the most extravagant example of Elia's protean nature and Lamb's versatile role-playing, given its embodiment of five strikingly different personae, each with its distinctive voice, its distinctive prose style. Elia first appears in the guise of a culinary historian, who in proper scholarly fashion begins by citing a Chinese manuscript, interpreted by "his friend M.," as the source of his upcoming story about the origin of roast pig. Though Elia's account of how Ho-ti and Bo-bo stumble upon the method is ludicrously developed, Elia maintains a deadpan style of exposition from the starting episode — when Bo-bo accidentally burns down the family cottage and "a litter of new-farrowed pigs," the aroma of which "assailed his nostrils, unlike any scent which he had before experienced" — to his concluding scholarly citation, "By such slow degrees, concludes the manuscript, do the most useful, and seemingly the most obvious arts, make their way among mankind." Having concluded his mock-scholarly role, Elia suddenly morphs into a high-flown enthusiastic celebrant of roast pig, "Of all the delicacies in the whole *mundus edibilis*, I will maintain it to be the most delicate—*princeps obsonorium*." And several hundred words later, he is still in the epideictic mode, ardently balancing one clause with another: "Pig—let me speak his praise—is not less provocative of the appetite, than he is satisfactory to the criticalness of the censorious palate. The strong man may batten on him, and the weakling refuseth not his mild juices." But then just as suddenly as Elia had switched from culinary historian to culinary celebrant, he morphs into yet another persona, in this case a personal essayist or culinary memoirist, vowing that he would never relinquish a pig that came into his hands, a vow occasioned by the sorrowful recollection of an episode in his life when the salute of "a gray-headed old beggar" led him in a fit of misplaced charity to give away "a smoking plum-cake, fresh from the oven" that had been baked for him by his "good old aunt," who would be "disappointed . . . that I had never had a bite of it in my mouth at last." In this case, however, Lamb was not impersonating anyone but himself, for the episode constitutes an expanded version of the very same memory that Lamb had shared with Coleridge in a letter (March 20, 1822) written six months before the "Dissertation" was published (September 1822). Though the episode is relatively brief—no more than a few hundred words in length—its personal idiom, evocative detail, and expressive voice stand out by virtue of their sharp contrast with the other personae, particularly that of the culinary ethicist who appears immediately after the memoirist, pondering the question, "Whether, supposing that the flavour of a pig who obtained his death by whipping (*per flagellationem extremam*) superadded a pleasure upon the palate of a man more intense than any possible suffering we can conceive in the animal, is man justified in using that method of putting the animal to death?" One final voice—that of a chef with a few pithy flavoring suggestions—and the dissertation is done.

Given such a cacophony of voices, one can hardly resist the question of which one contains the truth, or where Lamb stands in the piece as a whole, or whether at last it is simply a jeu d'esprit, occasioned by his love of roast pig. It's tempting, of course, to suppose that Lamb can be heard most clearly in the passage that most clearly echoes the personal voice and recollection of his letter to Coleridge, but it's well to remember that in the essays of Elia, the playful and the serious, the whimsical and the thoughtful are often inseparable. So, after all, the other voices cannot be silenced, not only because of their distinctive styles but also because each bears witness in its way to a compelling truth, whether it's the hunger to imagine how our ancient forbears might have discovered or invented the methods of cooking that we most prize, or the necessity to consider the pain we inflict for the food that we savor, or the compulsion to express one's enthusiasm for the thing itself. All of which is to say that while Lamb is most clearly present in Elia's personal recollection, he is in his way as fully present in each of his other impersonations. In this respect, it might well be said that Lamb anticipates in his pseudonymous fashion the paradoxical dictum of Virginia Woolf: "never to be yourself, and yet always."

NEVER TO BE YOURSELF AND YET ALWAYS

Virginia Woolf on the Essayist's Problem

On November 30, 1922, the essay had a day in the sun, thanks to the *Times Literary Supplement*, whose lead article, "Modern Essays," filled the front page and part of the second—prominence rarely accorded an essay on the essay. Written by Virginia Woolf—anonymously, as then the custom in *TLS*—it was occasioned by the publication of *Modern English Essays*, a five-volume collection edited by Ernest Rhys, essayist, poet, and founder of the Everyman's Library Series. But Woolf made no pretense of reviewing his work. Aside from nodding at Rhys in her opening sentence, she mentions his collection only two or three times, using it instead as a sourcebook for taking stock of the modern essay: "as we turn over the pages of these five little volumes, containing essays written between 1870 and 1920, certain principles appear to control the chaos, and we detect in the short period under review something like the progress of history." But literary history was not Woolf's only concern. She also chose to have her say about the very nature and purpose of the essay. Casting her ideas in bold definitions and sweeping generalizations, she produced a piece that combines a historical survey with a virtual poetics of the essay, centered on a paradoxical relationship between essayists and their essayistic personae: "Never to be yourself and yet always—that is the problem." Front-page material indeed—so notable that three years later Woolf included it slightly revised in *The Common Reader* and retitled "The Modern Essay."

Positing such a problematic relationship between essayists and their essayistic selves may now seem commonplace, given postmodern literary theory and reflections on role-playing by such varied personal essayists as Nora Ephron, Edward Hoagland, Phillip Lopate, Nancy Mairs, Joyce Carol Oates, Scott Russell Sanders, and E. B. White. In Woolf's time, however, essayistic pretense was so uncommon a notion that she and others routinely equated Lamb with his Elian persona. Hardly surprising, then, that she only arrived at a more problematic conception after turning out some three hundred reviews and essays. She certainly did not inherit such a view from her father, Leslie Stephen, who in 1881 produced a lively but simplistic survey of English essayists, discussing their works as literal reflections of character and temperament. Nor would she have found a more nuanced view in Rhys, who discusses the essays in the general introduction to his collection as products of "a vagabond and free spirit" in "an increasingly natural mode"—in other words, as one and the same with the essayists who produced them. The handful of pieces in Rhys's collection which deal with individual essayists are similarly predisposed, in one case going so far as to express a keen sense of disappointment that Hazlitt's writing did not live up to reports of his conversational eloquence. Such a widespread inclination to view essays as would-be (or should-be) embodiments of their authors—a three-hundred year tradition, in fact—it's hardly surprising that Woolf herself was initially predisposed toward such an equation.

In her first piece on the subject, "The Decay of Essay Writing" (1905), Woolf made a special point of highlighting its personal element:

> Almost all essays begin with a capital I—"I think," "I feel"—
> and when you have said that, it is clear that you are not writing
> history or philosophy or biography or anything but an essay,
> which may be brilliant or profound, which may deal with
> the immortality of the soul, or the rheumatism in your left
> shoulder, but is primarily an expression of personal opinion.

Though it might be brilliant or profound, "an expression of personal opinion" would probably have sounded to Woolf's readers like a falling-off from the substance and rigors of history, philosophy, and biography. Lest there be any doubt about her discomfort with personal opinion, Woolf made it explicit in her assertion that the essay "owes its popularity to the fact that its proper use is to express one's personal peculiarities, so that under the decent veil of print one can indulge one's egoism to the full." Woolf was troubled, in part, by the "immense" popularity of the personal essay and by what she perceived to be its "amazing" egoism. But she was equally disturbed by the proliferation of familiar essays about music, art, and literature—armchair criticism, in other words, that did not embody any special knowledge or insight but was "simply the expression of such individual likes and dislikes — the amiable garrulity of the tea table." Yet Woolf was not so averse to the personal element as to rule it out completely. Later in the same piece, she envisioned a memoir-like essay devoted entirely to personal experience (rather than personal opinion), with such a deliberate focus on the self that it might well be considered a rationale for the interiorized essays of our time:

> If men and women must write, let them leave the great mysteries of art and literature unassailed; if they told us frankly not of the books that we can all read and the pictures which hang for us all to see, but of that single book to which they alone have the key and of that solitary picture whose face is shrouded to all but one gaze — if they would write of themselves — such writing would have its own permanent value.

While the image of a "solitary picture whose face is shrouded to all but one gaze" suggests not just a deeply private self but also a distinctly different public self—a bifurcation that would profoundly influence her fictional concerns and narrative techniques—Woolf did not at that point expand upon the duality or its implications. For no sooner did she envision such an intensely personal essay than she soured at the few examples of it in her own time, finding them either deficient "in the cardinal virtue of sincerity" or beset by "amazing and unclothed egoism." Woolf, it seems, had such a refined conception of appropriate essayistic conduct that hardly anyone could live up to it — "no one," she proclaimed, "has approached the essays of Elia."

It's tempting to attribute such harsh judgments to the perfectionism (or intolerance) of youth, but in the years that followed Woolf continued to take her fellow essayists to task, sometimes for their "egotistical diversions," sometimes for their "melodious meditations," sometimes for their "imitative essays," sometimes for their "dance upon the tight rope." Reviewing a collection by Robert Lynd, whose work had first appeared in the *New Statesman*, she began with a scathing set of reflections on "the lighter form of essay" that typically provided a diversion of sorts from "the politics" of a "serious sixpenny weekly." Woolf was so put off by the acrobatics of such essays that she evidently had not sampled Lynd's newspaper pieces until they appeared in book form, and thus she was pleasantly surprised to find him "so competent a writer that we need have no fear that he is going to break his bones." Yet no sooner did Woolf acknowledge his "literary skill," as well as his "open and generous mind," than she disparaged Lynd for suppressing "what we take to be the chief stock-in-trade of the essayist—himself. It is a most serious omission." Here, then, in 1918, as in her earlier piece, she highlighted the essayist's self as the essential element of the form and in this case went so far as to doubt "whether a first-rate essay has ever been written which is not the ripe fruit of egoism." A seeming reversal of her prior distress with egoism in the essay. But in this instance, Woolf equated the egoism of exemplary essayists not with excessive self-regard but with appropriate self-revelation:

> The essays of Elia are so many confidences which impart to us the most private secrets of Lamb's heart. There is room in them for all sorts of facts about his whims and habits, but there is very little concern for the public good. The most delightful parts of Montaigne's essays are those where he breaks from the consideration of some abstract quality to explore the peculiarities of his body or his soul. It is the same with Hazlitt, or with Thackeray in the *Roundabout Papers*. None of these men has the least fear of giving himself away, and perhaps, in a short piece that is the only thing of value one can give away.

I have quoted this passage at length to highlight Woolf's amplification of her previous urging that essayists "write of themselves," "of that solitary picture whose face is shrouded to all but one gaze." Though it might seem hyperbolic to assert, even provisionally, that self-revelation "is the only thing of value" an essayist "can give away," Woolf was not alone in that seeming conviction. A. C. Benson, whose piece on the essay appeared in the fifth volume of Rhys's collection just a few years later, also insisted that though "a man must not wear his heart upon his sleeve . . . that is just what the essayist must do." Despite such emphatic assertions, that is not what English essayists of the time were actually doing. Neither Woolf nor the authors in Rhys's collection bear witness to "the most private secrets" of their hearts, except in moments so infrequent as to make one all the more conscious of their manifest intent to be sociable and polite—qualities that do not induce one "to explore the peculiarities of his body or his soul." Even in "Impressions of Leslie Stephen," a brief essay about her father, published in 1906, two years after he died, Woolf immersed herself so much in the matter-of-fact details of his nightly readings that she concealed herself almost completely. Indeed, as if to mock the very idea of self-revelation, Max Beerbohm turned himself into a chameleon of sorts and became one of the most admired essayists of his time. So, perhaps, it's not surprising that during the next few years Woolf evidently rethought her conception of the essayist's persona, resulting in a distinctly different conviction about the essayist's imperative.

Two years after her piece on Lynd, Woolf wrote such an ecstatic review of Beerbohm's collection, *And Even Now*, that she virtually abandoned the role of critic: "Are there still to be found reviewers who review Mr. Beerbohm. . . . The truth is plain. Mr. Beerbohm is reviewing us." Beerbohm, according to Woolf, soared above the realm of criticism, and thus she titled her piece "A Flying Lesson." A notably rare and enthusiastic affirmation for someone given to such harsh criticism of her fellow essayists. Notable too for its celebration of a writer so inclined to role-playing — from his epistolary put-downs in "How Shall I Word It?" to his Maupassantian manner in "A Relic" to his antiquarian posturing in "Quia Imperfectum" — that one might wonder whether he ever gave himself away, even in such apparently sincere pieces as "No. 2 The Pines" and "Something Defeasible," or whether sincerity itself was a role that he played. A distinctly different kind of essayistic gift from the one that Woolf had espoused in her review of Lynd, so different as to suggest that in praising Beerbohm she had tacitly abandoned the naïve equation of essayist and essayistic persona that informed her previous commentary and reviews, foreshadowing the problematic conception she openly espoused two years later in "Modern Essays" — "never to be yourself, and yet always; that is the problem." Neither her letters nor her diaries of that period give any hint of Woolf's changing thoughts about the essay, but the shifting consciousness of the characters she portrayed in *Night and Day* (1919) and the disconnect she depicted between their surface expressions and their inner life clearly suggest that in her fiction of the time Woolf was already exploring the problematic interplay of the self in public and the self in thought.

Woolf's extravagant review of *And Even Now* was a harbinger of things to come, for two years later in "Modern Essays," she not only dubbed Beerbohm the "prince of his profession" but also featured him in an extended discussion comprising the heart of her essay. Beerbohm was so touched by her lavish praise and attention that in a letter to Woolf challenging her modernist agenda (December 30, 1927), he went out of his way to thank her for being "nice about my essays." According to Woolf's historical overview, the style and content of Beerbohm's essays made an important break from the stentorian purposefulness of the Victorians, returning in effect to the more intimate voice and personal subject matter of Montaigne and Lamb: "Thus, sometime in the nineties, it must have surprised readers accustomed to exhortation, information, and denunciation to find themselves familiarly addressed by a voice which seemed to belong to a man no larger than themselves." More important to Woolf than Beerbohm's personable voice was his deliberate intent, as she perceived it, to make personality a major element of his essays, as if it were something that could be self-consciously implemented and manipulated: "Once again we have an essayist capable of using the essayist's most proper but most dangerous and delicate tool. He has brought personality into literature, not unconsciously and impurely, but so consciously and purely that we do not know whether there is any relation between Max the essayist and Mr. Beerbohm the man."

By positing such a clear-cut distinction between the essayist and the man, the persona and the person, Woolf moved far afield from her tacit equation of the two in reviewing Lynd, particularly given her uncertainty about the existence of any relation between the two. And then having boldly separated the two, she brought them together in a paradoxical yoking that marks the conceptual high point of her reflections on Beerbohm and the essayist's distinctive challenge: "We only know that the spirit of personality permeates every word that he writes. The triumph is the triumph of style. For it is only by knowing how to write that you can make use in literature of your self; that self which, while it is essential to literature, is also its most dangerous antagonist. Never to be yourself and yet always—that is the problem." Woolf's emphatic connection of personality with style, with knowing how to write, clearly makes it the product of art and artifice rather than an unrehearsed emanation of the self. Her double-edged view of the self accounts for both her paradoxical definition of the essayist's problem and the imperative of solving it through artistic control. And lest there be any questions about her rationale for crafting one's self through the discipline of style, she answers with some withering remarks about essayists in Rhys's collection who have failed to do so: "We are nauseated by the sight of trivial personalities decomposing in the eternity of print. As talk, no doubt, it was charming. . . . But literature is stern; it is no use being charming, virtuous, or even learned and brilliant into the bargain, unless, she seems to reiterate, you fulfill her first condition—to know how to write."

It goes without saying, of course, that one must know how to write in producing an essay or any other form of literature. Yet Woolf felt compelled to reiterate that self-evident truth, for she deemed it a unique imperative of the essay, as she makes clear early on in her piece: "A novel has a story, a poem rhyme; but what art can the essayist use in these short lengths of prose? He must know—that is the first essential—how to write." Knowing how to write was such an important matter for Woolf that she made it a leitmotif of "The Modern Essay," sounding that theme not only in her celebration of Beerbohm but also in critiques of his predecessors and contemporaries. Given such an intense concern with how to write, Woolf paid attention to all the elements of style, from word choice to tone of voice, laying down rules with magisterial assurance: "Of all forms of literature, the essay is the one which least calls for the use of long words. . . . Literal truth-telling and finding fault with a culprit for his good are out of place in an essay. . . . But if the voice of the scold should never be heard in this narrow plot, there is another voice which is as a plague of locusts—the voice of a man stumbling among loose words, clutching aimlessly at vague ideas." As these passages suggest, Woolf believed that knowing how to write involved not just a mastery of craft but an exquisite sense of tact, for she ultimately believed that the quality and success of an essay depends above all else on the illusion of an engaging and genial personality. Her intense belief in the importance of personality led her to worry even about the increasing number and shrinking length of essays:

> Where Lamb wrote one essay and Max perhaps writes two,
> Mr. Belloc at a rough computation produces three hundred and

sixty-five. They are very short, it is true. . . . But the personality upon which Mr. Belloc, like Mr. Beerbohm, depends suffers in the process. It comes to us not with the natural richness of the speaking voice, but strained and thin and full of mannerisms and affectations, like the voice of a man shouting through a megaphone to a crowd on a windy day.

The illusion of authenticity was clearly for Woolf the sine qua non, so much so that it led her to formulate one of the most striking and haunting pronouncements in her piece:

> to write like oneself and call it not writing is a much harder exercise than to write like Addison and Steele and call it writing well.

When I first encountered this passage — which comes at the end of an extended contrast between the plain style of Samuel Butler and the polished prose of Robert Louis Stevenson — I assumed that "to write like oneself" was an idiomatic expression for writing in one's natural manner, in other words, without affectation. But the more I thought about that phrase, the more it puzzled me, for I didn't understand how a natural way of writing could be more difficult than writing like Addison. Nor could I understand why one would choose to "call it not writing." Then it occurred to me that Woolf might have used that phrase to indicate an unusual kind of imitation, not of someone else but of oneself. How strange, I thought, to engage in such an activity, as if one's self could be embodied in writing only by a bizarre kind of imitation, not of someone else but of oneself. As if one were compelled to engage in something like a schizophrenic distancing of oneself from oneself, so as to arrive at a conception of oneself, or of one's writing, that one might then imitate, so as "to write like oneself." How bold, in turn, not only to engage in such a deliberately self-imitative activity but also to "call it not writing," as if it were nothing out of the ordinary, an unself-conscious thing — just being oneself. No wonder that Woolf considered it "a much harder exercise than to write like Addison and call it writing well." Strange as such a pretense might seem, it reflects an impulse similar to Montaigne's desire "to be seen in my simple, natural, ordinary fashion." An artful artlessness that has often characterized the personal essay and often been so convincing as to be taken at face value, as if the essayist's persona were not a verbal illusion but the essayist in person, the author plain and simple. Indeed, in the wake of Montaigne, more than three centuries of commentators made that literal-minded equation before Woolf explicitly defined the pretense in her discussion of Beerbohm.

The magical appeal of such an illusion emerges most vividly in Woolf's remarkable personification of literary texts: "Even things in a book-case change if they are alive; we find ourselves wanting to meet them again; we find them altered. So we look back upon essay after essay by Mr. Beerbohm, knowing that, come September or May, we shall sit down with them and talk." The premise of this passage—that essays can be "alive" and thus be as changeable as human beings—is, of course, outlandish. A conceit extraordinaire, unparalleled in prior commentary on the personal essay, especially given its corollary, that one can "sit down with them and talk." As if an essay were so animated by the vividness of its author's persona as to be a virtual (or actual!) person. Yet Woolf develops the conceit in such a matter-of-fact way, without a hint of irony, that she endows it with the force of a literal truth. Perhaps because it does contain elements of truth, for the livelier and richer an essay, the more likely we are to find ourselves wanting to read it again and to see it differently on successive readings—"we find them altered." (And, one might add, we often find ourselves altered as well.) Besides, we do often talk with (or talk back to) essays in the process of reading them, as you might be even now. A silent conversation, yet a conversation nonetheless. Possibly wanting to tell me that I'm making more of Woolf's statement than she intended. But she made a special point of wording (or rather, rewording) it that way, for when the passage first appeared in the *Times Literary Supplement* (November 1922), she concluded it in a distinctly different fashion: "we shall return and start again as with people who have been living all the while." Though the gist of that analogy anticipates the conceit, it has none of the force that arises from the buried metaphor of the 1925 version she prepared for *The Common Reader*—"we shall sit down with them and talk." And that revision was one of only ten otherwise slight rewordings, most of them refinements in tone or idiom. But in this singular case, Woolf evidently wanted to animate the passage with a resonance of civilized conversation that she attributes to the experience of reading and responding to a lively essay.

Talk, civilized talk, is the essence Woolf evokes here, so it's not surprising that she reflects on its emblematic locus:

> The drawing-room is the place where a great deal of reading is done nowadays, and the essays of Mr. Beerbohm lie, with an exquisite appreciation of all that the position exacts, upon the drawing-room table. There is no gin about; no strong tobacco; no puns, drunkenness, or insanity. Ladies and gentlemen talk together, and some things, of course, are not said.

Woolf's vivid evocation of the drawing-room ambiance reminds one that it was, after all, a very confined and confining place—so far from the hurly-burly of ordinary experience as to be a world apart. A world of ladies and gentlemen, if you please, which suggests that in lionizing Beerbohm and espousing "the spirit of personality," Woolf tacitly privileged a socially elite persona and by extension a repressive conception of the essay, where some things, of course, are not mentioned—certainly not subjects close to the bone. And therein lies the problem with her idea of the essay—albeit path-breaking in its paradoxical conception of the essayist's challenge, it is, at last, profoundly inhibited, and not just in its drawing-room norms for the essayist's persona but also in its escapist conception of the essayist's purpose, which she enunciates early in her piece:

> The principle which controls it is simply that it should give pleasure; the desire which impels us when we take it from the shelf is simply to receive pleasure. Everything in an essay must be subdued to that end. It should lay us under a spell with its first word, and we should only wake, refreshed, with its last. In the interval we may pass through the most various experiences of amusement, surprise, interest, indignation; we may soar to the heights of fantasy with Lamb or plunge to the depths of wisdom with Bacon, but we must never be roused. The essay must lap us about and draw its curtain across the world.

When I first pondered that provocative statement some forty years ago, I was teaching a course called "Art of the Essay" and working on a textbook introduction to the essay as a form of literature—

in both cases eager to expand the academic study of essays beyond the pragmatic and solemn necessities of introductory composition by making a rationale for their inclusion in the world of literary forms. So I was delighted to hear Woolf speak of the essay as one of the "forms of literature," whose controlling "principle . . . is simply that it should give pleasure." Delighted as well by her affirmation of the "amusement, surprise, interest, indignation" that I too was experiencing as I made my way through essays by Annie Dillard, Joan Didion, Nora Ephron, Loren Eiseley, Edward Hoagland, E. B. White, and Tom Wolfe. What I couldn't fathom—or perhaps more accurately what I couldn't accept—was her subsequent assertion that the essay "should lay us under a spell with its first words, and we should only wake refreshed with its last," that it "must lap us about and draw its curtain across the world." How, I wondered, could such a trance-like, otherworldly state of mind—an imaginative escape of sorts—be induced by essays, given their frequent immersion in the world of human experience, messy and painful as it often is? But I didn't puzzle over that question very long, for in the very next paragraph, Woolf attributed its hypnotic force to "the magic of writing," a phrase that seemed to endow the essay with the imaginative power ordinarily attributed to literature—the very thing that I wanted to highlight in my textbook piece on the essay.

Since then, however, I've not been able to reread that passage or consider Woolf's essay as a whole without being brought up short by its escapist implications, especially because it was written just a few years after the end of the First World War, when one might suppose that the horrors and troubling aftermath of the war would have led her to a more existential view of the essayist's purpose. But Woolf was not alone in her thinking about the essay. The fifth volume of Rhys's collection, which covers the war years, begins with Arthur Clutton-Brock's celebration of "The Magic Flute," ends with Rhys's tribute to the travel and nature writing of W. H. Hudson, and in between offers engaging pieces by the likes of Galsworthy on hunting and Milne on intemperance. As if the war and the essay were worlds apart. In such a genteel collection it's not surprising to find that the fifth volume also includes Arthur Benson's "The Art of the Essayist," which asserts that "the essay need not concern itself with anything definite. . . . The only thing necessary is that the thing or the thought should be vividly apprehended, enjoyed, felt to be beautiful, and expressed with a certain gusto." All of which sounds like a watered-down version of art for art's sake. So, it might be said that Woolf's emphasis on pleasure was perfectly in keeping with the essay of her time and with the aesthetic views of Benson and others.

In the years that followed, Woolf evidently didn't change her mind about the essayist and the essay. Eight years after "Modern Essays," in a piece commemorating the hundredth anniversary of Hazlitt's death, she bluntly took him to task for being "emphatically himself":

> He has no reticence and he has no shame. He tells us
> exactly what he thinks, and he tells us — the confidence is
> less seductive — exactly what he feels. . . . So thin is the veil
> of the essay as Hazlitt wore it, his very look comes before
> us. We see him as Coleridge saw him, "brow- hanging, shoe-
> contemplative, strange."

Given such a fierce commitment to the essayist's veil, it's not surprising that shortly after her piece on Hazlitt (1930), Woolf veiled herself in "On Being Ill," which opens with her well-known wonderment at the absence of literary writing on illness but then barely hints at the mental and physical illnesses that bedeviled her throughout her life. "Some things, of course, are not said" but reserved for one's diaries. More than fifty years and another world war would pass before essayists began to abandon the veil and Joan Didion produced such pieces as "In Bed" and "The White Album," vividly detailing her physical and mental illness. But that is another story, befitting a separate piece called "Illness and 'I': Malady in the Personal Essay."

Personae and Culture

DIFFERENCE AND "I"

Cultural Consciousness in the Personal Essay

For much of its history, the personal essay has been a domain of white male authors, so inattentive to the drastically different circumstances of women and minorities that Lamb's diatribe on the mistreatment of women stands out as a premodern rarity. Far from speaking out on cultural and political issues, personal essayists from Montaigne to Beerbohm chose to ruminate instead on books, ideas, manners, and personal experience. So, the "I" of the personal essay often echoed its genial and peaceable settings—the book-lined study, the coffee house, the drawing room, the rural retreat—settings attuned to a persona that was companionable rather than contentious, reflective rather than assertive, witty rather than solemn. In other words, a charming, white male of yore without any ax to grind. The appeal of that personage was once so strong that as late as 1918, Agnes Repplier, America's then most notable female essayist, affirmed it in her assertion that the essayist's "personality is born of leisure and reflection"—not of such "bitter and blinding truths" that come in a time of war. It's not surprising, then, that Virginia Woolf frowned on the discontented manner of Hazlitt and celebrated the chameleon-like Beerbohm as the early twentieth century's preeminent essayist. Though the traditionally charming "I" would make one more distinguished appearance in the essays of E. B. White, the contemporaneous essays of George Orwell embodied such an intense consciousness of colonialized cultures and subjugated people that they prefigured a radical change in the essayist's persona. Indeed, when blacks, Latinos, Native Americans, and women came to write of their personal experiences, they often did so by directly confronting the differences that set them apart or the tensions and abuse provoked by such difference, as in Richard Wright's "The Ethics of Living Jim Crow," a searing account of the abuse that he suffered from white fellow laborers during his early working years. In pieces with such a focus, the essayist's intense concern with painful experience inevitably leads to a drastically different persona from the genial companion of the past.

I remember my first encounter with such a presence in James Baldwin's "Stranger in a Village," which I read some fifty years ago, when I was a teaching assistant, guiding my freshman students through the more familiar terrain of Bacon, Addison, Lamb, Beerbohm, and White. Baldwin's persona was so imbued with an intense consciousness of difference that it seemed completely at odds with those traditional essayists. As its title suggests, Baldwin's essay centers on his experience in a Swiss mountaintop village where "no black man had ever set foot . . . before I came." A bizarre sojourn for Baldwin who never imagined "that there could be people anywhere who had never seen a Negro." Also bizarre for the villagers, whose naïve curiosity about his physical traits led them to treat him like a freak of nature rather than a human being, as Baldwin makes clear in a striking series of recollections:

> Some thought my hair was the color of tar, that it had the texture of wire, or the texture of cotton. It was jocularly suggested that I might let it grow long and make myself a winter coat. If I sat in the sun for more than five minutes some daring creature was certain to come along and gingerly put his fingers on my hair, as though he were afraid of an electric shock, or put his hand on my hand, astonished that the color did not rub off. In all of this, in which it must be conceded there was the charm of genuine wonder, and in which there was certainly no element of intentional unkindness, there was yet no suggestion that I was human. I was simply a living wonder.
>
> I knew that they did not mean to be unkind, and I know it now; it is necessary, nevertheless, for me to repeat this to myself each time that I walk out of the chalet.

Here as elsewhere in the first part of this essay, Baldwin looks at the villagers looking at him, or one might say that his persona emerges through a sustained concentration upon "I" as perceived by "They," as well as a reciprocal concentration on "They" as perceived by "I." "I" vis-à-vis "They." Though my focus on those pronouns has the effect of schematizing this vivid and evocative passage, it serves to highlight a significant pattern that distinguishes Baldwin's essay from traditional pieces in which the persona typically develops through a concentration upon itself at different times in its life—the I-present versus the I-past, the self remembering versus the remembered self, as in White's "Once More to the Lake" or Didion's "On Keeping a Notebook." By contrast, Baldwin's "I" is so preoccupied with "They" as to suggest at first that his persona is in a sense inseparable from the villagers—one might even say in thrall to them, given his obsessive concern with their perception and treatment of him. Baldwin's "I" subsequently engages in such a thoughtful analysis of the interplay that his persona ultimately comes across as a compelling interpreter of the cultural situation:

> I say that the culture of these people controls me—but they can scarcely be held responsible for European culture. America comes out of Europe, but these people have never seen America, nor have most of them seen more of Europe than the hamlet at the foot of their mountains. Yet they move with an authority which I shall never have; and they regard me, quite rightly, not only as a stranger in their village but as a suspect latecomer, bearing no credentials, to everything they have—however unconsciously—inherited.
>
> For this village, even were it incomparably more remote and incredibly more primitive, is the West, the West onto which I have been so strangely grafted.

The absence of complaint is notable throughout, and its absence contributes to the intellectual self-control that characterizes Baldwin's persona, as he moves inexorably from the particulars of his experience with the villagers to a historical overview and analysis of the black American experience that culminates in a striking declaration of his overriding concern: "the interracial drama acted out on the American continent has not only created a new black man, it has created a new white man, too. No road whatever will lead Americans back to the simplicity of this European village where white men still have the luxury of looking on me as a stranger." Thus an essay that began in a vividly personal manner gradually turns into a cultural history and critique that reaches its climax in an overarching generalization about race relations in America. And Baldwin's persona undergoes a similar transformation, the "I" at the start gradually giving way to a culturally charged third-person perspective.

A shift in perspective also takes place in Alice Walker's 1967 essay, "The Civil Rights Movement: What Good Was It?"—written during a time when many liberal whites were questioning the accomplishments of the civil rights movement. As her title suggests, Walker, like Baldwin, is concerned with intercultural perceptions. But rather than beginning like Baldwin in the mode of a personal essayist, Walker completely suppresses any reference to herself, opening instead with a vivid anecdote about an "old lady," a "legendary freedom fighter," who when told that the movement was dead archly replied, "if it's dead, it shore ain't ready to lay down." Having established her view of the movement without mentioning herself, Walker then reviews the contrary perceptions of disenchanted liberals:

> Still, white liberals and deserting Civil Rights sponsors are quick to justify their disaffection from the Movement by claiming that it is over. . . . They then list statistics supposedly showing how much more advanced segregation is now than ten years ago—in schools, housing, jobs. They point to a gain in conservative politicians during the last few years. They speak of ghetto riots and of the survey that shows that most politicians are admittedly too anti-Negro to do their jobs in ghetto areas fairly and effectively. They speak of every area that has been touched by the Civil Rights Movements as somehow or other going to pieces.

In this paragraph as in the next, Walker focuses relentlessly on "they" with nary a single "I" to interrupt her focus. Maintaining her focus on "they," she turns from summarizing their claims to itemizing their oversights:

> They rarely talk, however, about human attitudes among Negroes that have undergone terrific changes just during the past seven to ten years (not to mention all those years when there was a Movement and only the Negroes knew about it). They seldom speak of changes in personal lives because of the influence of people in the Movement. . . . They have apparently never stopped to wonder why it is always the white man—on his radio and in his newspaper and on his television—who says that the Movement is dead.

By this point, Walker's persona sounds like a skillful debater, given her pointed opening anecdote, followed by the methodical acknowledgment of opposing views and rebuttal of the opposition. But Walker's rhetorical persona gradually gives way to a self-revelatory "I," when she tells about the listlessness of her existence before "the Civil Rights Movement came into my life."

> It was just six years ago that I began to be alive. I had, of
> course, been living before — for I am now twenty-three — but
> I did not really know it. And I did not know it because nobody
> told me that I — a pensive, yearning, typical high school senior,
> but Negro — existed in the minds of others as I existed in
> my own. Until that time my mind was locked apart from the
> outer contours and complexion as if my mind and body were
> strangers.

In the course of this reminiscence, Walker bears witness not only to her own psychological privations but also to those of her mother, who was evidently so addicted to the televised soap operas of white American life that "She placed herself in every scene she saw, with her braided hair turned blond, her two hundred pounds compressed into a sleek size-seven dress, her rough dark skin smooth and *white*." In this haunting account of wishfulfillment, Walker's personal "I" becomes a painfully astute cultural and psychological observer: "my mother, a maid for nearly forty years, never once identified herself with the scarcely glimpsed black servant's face beneath the ruffled cap. Like everyone else, in her daydreams at least, she thought she was free." But when Walker tells about the moment she beheld Martin Luther King on TV—"the first black face I saw on our new television screen"—she becomes an impassioned acolyte: "I fell in love with the sober and determined face of the Movement." And the passion builds through the remainder of the essay, in which she tells about her personal transformation, then about the manifold transformations in black American life resulting from the movement, then about "the hippies and other nihilists" who deny the efficacy of the movement while "tripping" on drugs, and then about the movement itself, which "broke the pattern of black servitude" and "shattered the phony 'promise' of white soap operas that sucked away so many pitiful lives." Thus her personal "I" is framed by an argumentative third-person presence that becomes increasingly eloquent, concluding with a memorably brief sentence in first-person plural that echoes her opening anecdote: "Because we live, it can never die."

By contrast with Baldwin and Walker, Annie Dillard writes about her confrontation with difference from an unwaveringly first-person point of view in "The Deer at Providencia," a piece occasioned by her discovery that while watching a roped deer in an Ecuadorian village "trying to paw itself free," her three male traveling companions had been intently watching her. "I" vis-à-vis "They" once again:

> They all said that I had no expression on my face when I was watching the deer — or at any rate, not the expression they expected.
>
> They had looked to see how I, the only woman, and the youngest was taking the deer's struggles. I looked detached, apparently, or hard, or calm, or focused, still.

Dillard's facial expression, it seems, had completely challenged the men's stereotyped expectations of how a woman might respond to such a spectacle of suffering, her visibly calm behavior so contrary to their expectations that she and they "stayed up all that night talking" about it. In recollecting a bit of the conversation, Dillard reveals the impassioned response the men had expected of her (and, by implication, the dispassionate, self-controlled reaction they attributed to themselves):

> "If it had been my wife," one man said with special vigor, amazed, "she wouldn't have cared *what* was going on; she would have dropped *everything* right at that moment and gone in the village from here to there to there, she would not have *stopped* until that animal was out of its suffering one way or another. She couldn't *bear* to see a creature in agony like that."

Dillard's prior account of witnessing the deer suggests that rather than behaving like her companions' stereotype of the hysterically compassionate woman, she was apparently not the impassive spectator they had perceived her to be. Indeed, Dillard's account suggests that she was fascinated by the hopeless situation of the deer, watching it struggle for some fifteen minutes rather than quickly turning away as she could easily have done. Thus she details its struggles like a dispassionate naturalist. But it's not my intent to establish how Dillard appeared or behaved in Providencia. What compels my interest is her sustained projection of a fiercely independent "I," refusing to be tethered by the rope of her companions' chauvinistic preconceptions, as reflected in her dramatic apostrophe: "Gentlemen of the city, what surprises you? That there is suffering here, or that I know it?" Even more striking is the fact that though Dillard and her companions stayed up talking all night, she reports so little of the conversation—nothing but the one man's surmise of how his wife would have reacted to the suffering deer—that she apparently aims to present herself as being above it all. An "I" who treats the white male "They" with contemptuous brevity in the two-word report of her reaction to the man's story: "I nodded." Her story, she seems to imply, speaks for itself. Thus she does not use it as an emblematic point of reference in an extended argument, which might well have undermined the persona that emanates from her studied brevity.

Though Dillard's understated manner differs markedly from the impassioned oratorical stance of Walker which differs in turn from the culturally charged voice of Baldwin, it's well to keep in mind that such varied personae emanate from the archetypal situation of "I" vis-à-vis "They" (or "We" vis-à-vis "They" as in Walker's piece)—a situation that seems to involve something like a rhetorical catch-22. For no matter how the "I" might seek to assert its independence from "They," the very act of claiming its independence (or indifference, as in Dillard's piece) necessarily requires that the "I" define itself vis-à-vis "They" rather than by reference to itself alone or to someone or something other than "They." Or to put the predicament in linguistic terms, as Gerald Early does in the preface to *Tuxedo Junction*, "for the Black essayist, sound must always try to be subversion, the slave's language is always undermining the master's tongue even as it imperfectly replicates it, even as it aspires to be the master's tongue." Even Dillard is unable to escape that predicament, though she tries to do so in the concluding segment of her piece:

When we walked by the deer at Providencia for the last time, I said to Pepe, with a pitying glance at the deer, "*Pobrecito*"— "poor little thing." But I was trying out Spanish. I knew at the time it was a ridiculous thing to say.

So it seems as if Dillard having been moved to pity for the deer, in a seemingly genuine outburst, reflexively feels compelled once again to refute the men's stereotype of women by dismissing her compassionate remark, but in doing so she comes across as being more tethered to their perceptions, more preoccupied with their view of things than she might wish to imply. The "I," after all, is tacitly defined by the way it comes to terms with "They."

The ineluctable nature of that catch-22 came home to me a few years ago when I thought about doing a piece on the occasion of my seventy-fifth birthday, having reached that notable age still vigorous enough to tend my garden and challenge myself on the treadmill four or five days a week. Not just a grand old man, thought I, but a healthy one as well. The only problem was that the myth of the grand old man had passed away before I reached that once-hallowed state, done in by the youth culture of our time. My gray hair no longer the emblem of an éminence grise but the telltale sign of a geezer, my aged vigor a trifle compared to the crackle of life in a university town, filled with people younger than I, jogging by, talking so much faster than I, that the speed of their chatter was—and still is—intimidating. Even for someone with digital hearing aids. And worse still, when I see that my slow-paced conversation tries their patience. Their language masters me, making me feel like a second-class citizen, unable to replicate the speed of their discourse. Do their minds really move as quickly as their mouths, or is it just an illusion, without the niceties of deliberation? And when, pray tell, did speed-talk come into fashion? Whatever the case, when it came time to do my piece on reaching seventy-five, I couldn't imagine writing about it without writing about them as well—"I" vis-à-vis "They"—, and I couldn't imagine writing about them without whining about the difference, as I seem to be doing right now. Perhaps I might have felt otherwise were I not living in a place where the young so outnumber the old that one can hardly avoid a sense of estrangement. But then it occurred to me that difference, after all, is universal, as ancient as the Garden of Eden. One needn't even be in a minority to feel it. Lamb was so alienated by the demonstrative affections of his married friends that he wrote "A Bachelor's Complaint Against Married Couples," and in a somewhat similar spirit Phillip Lopate produced "Against Joie de Vivre."

Given the challenge of writing about difference without being rhetorically oppressed by it, essayists have become increasingly resourceful in the ways they project themselves and their personal experience. In "Aria: A Memoir of a Bilingual Childhood," Richard Rodriguez begins by telling about the day when he "first entered a classroom" and immediately found himself the "problem student," given that all his "classmates were white and many were the children of doctors and lawyers and business executives," whereas his father was an immigrant laborer untutored in the language. "I" vis-à-vis "They," but rather than narrating this episode in a tone of anger or embarrassment, Rodriguez reports it in a matter-of-fact style, focusing on his exact perceptions of the moment rather than his feelings about the difference:

> The nun said, in a friendly but oddly impersonal voice: "Boys and girls, this is Richard Rodriguez." (I heard her sound it out—"*Rich-heard Road-ree-guess.*") It was the first time I heard anyone say my name in English.

And Rodriguez rarely diverges from this calm voice in telling about his language-learning experiences in and out of the classroom, thereby authenticating his ultimate mastery of the language. But he does assume other stances at various points throughout the essay.

Shortly after telling about his first classroom experience, Rodriguez suddenly shifts his temporal focus, "Now many years later, I hear of something called *bilingual education.*" And a bit later, he shifts from a first-person reportorial "I" into a third-person argumentative stance: "It is not possible for a child, *any* child, ever to use his family's language in school. Not to understand this is to misunderstand the public uses of schooling and to trivialize the nature of intimate life." A few sentences later, he's back in first-person, but a distinctly different "I" from the narrator of his classroom experience—in this case, a thoughtfully analytic self, looking back with compassionate understanding at the immigrant situation of his parents: "despite all they achieved, or perhaps because they had so much to achieve, they lacked any deep feeling of ease, of belonging in public. They regarded the people at work or in crowds as being very distant from us." So in a handful of opening paragraphs, Rodriguez uses three different stances and voices, which he interweaves throughout the remainder of his essay, sometimes turning the analytic perspective upon himself, sometimes using the reportorial stance to tell about his father's difficulties with English or the widening gap between himself and his parents that developed in the wake of his increasing mastery of English, but always using the argumentative voice to challenge the supporters of bilingual education. Different as those three voices may be, they share the rigors of a dispassionate, intellectualized view of things, ultimately concerned with making a case for an immigrant child's mastery of English and a corollary argument that familial intimacy does not necessarily reside in a native language but in the persons who utter such words and the contexts of their utterance. Thus Rodriguez's aria never turns into a complaint against "they" and the word "gringo" is never uttered in resentment or scorn.

In "The Story of My Body," Judith Ortiz Cofer also confronts the problem of difference in a dispassionate manner, largely by means of a relentlessly matter-of-fact style, somewhat like Rodriguez's restrained account of his first day in school. Indeed, throughout her essay, Cofer reports her experience in such a calm manner that it seems as if she is deliberately trying to avoid emotional wording or judgmental phrasing. A difficult task, given that she writes about harassment from start to finish in a first-person point of view:

> I was born a white girl in Puerto Rico, but became a brown girl when I came to live in the United States. . . . My first experience of color prejudice occurred in a supermarket in Paterson, New Jersey. It was Christmastime, and I was eight or nine years old. . . . As with the color of my skin, I didn't consciously think about my height or size until other people made an issue of it. . . . It was in the playground and sports fields that my size-related problems began.

In these as in other passages, Cofer projects the informational voice of someone who might have been writing a case history rather than a vividly detailed memoir of the abuse she experienced because of her physical appearance. But unlike Rodriguez's early announcement and subsequent development of his argumentative thesis, Cofer does not broach the point of her story until the last few sentences of the piece:

My skin color, my size, and my appearance were variables—things that were judged according to my current self-image, the aesthetic values of the times, the places I was in, and the people I met. My studies, later my writing, the respect of the people who saw me as an individual person they cared about, these were the criteria for my sense of self-worth that I would concentrate on in my adult life.

The calmness with which Cofer announces even such a deeply held conviction, after withholding it throughout the entire essay, constitutes perhaps the most convincing evidence of her success in dealing with the rhetorical challenges of writing about difference.

Gerald Early by contrast doesn't hesitate to make his convictions clear in "Living with Daughters: Watching the Miss America Pageant." At the opening, for example, after confessing to "a certain amount of shamefacedness" for watching the Miss America contest every year with his wife and daughters, Early explains the source of his embarrassment in a sentence that begins calmly in first person but shifts into a fierce third person critique with the deft unfolding of a predicate clause: "The source of my embarrassment is that this program remains, despite its attempt in recent years to modernize its frightfully antique quality of 'women on parade,' a kind of maddeningly barbarous example of the persistent, hard, crass urge to sell." Here as elsewhere in his essay, Early combines first- and third-person points of view in a single sentence, moving so adroitly from one to the other that the segue seems almost invisible. And the sentence continues for some eighty more words of cultural criticism, climaxing in Early's assertion that "the program has all the cheap earnestness of a social uplift project being played as a musical revue in Las Vegas." Early goes on to make clear that his concern with the pageant is occasioned not just by its embodiment of "the worst sort of 'Americanism,' the soft smile of sex and the hard sell of toothpaste and hair dye ads wrapped in the dreamy ideological gauze of 'making it through one's own effort.'" Much more disturbing to him are the issues it raises about race, empowerment, and "race pride"—issues that he explores by interpreting the reactions of his wife and his daughters to such a traditionally white extravaganza, as well as by reflecting on such related matters as the hair-straightening practices of black women that he remembers watching as a boy:

> I can remember hearing my sisters' hair sizzle and crackle
> as the comb passed through with a kind of pungent smell of
> actually burning hair. And I, like an intentional moth, with
> lonely narrow arcs, hovered near this flame of femininity with
> fascinated impertinence. Had I witnessed the debilitating
> nullity of absence or was it the affirmation of an inescapable
> presence? Had I witnessed a mutilation or a rite of devotion?
> Black women's hair is, I decided even as a boy, unintelligible.
> And now I wonder, is the acceptance of the reigns of black
> women as Miss America a sign that black beauty has become
> part of the mainstream culture. Is the black woman now truly
> a presence?

In passages such as this, Early achieves a distinctive synthesis of personal recollection and cultural interpretation, resulting in an "I" that transcends a potential obsession with "They" by reconceiving the tension between the two as an intellectual problem involving a series of provocative questions rather than a set of complaints to be itemized. On the other hand, near the end of the essay in describing the pleasure that he and his wife experience upon witnessing the third black to win the title of Miss America, he doesn't hesitate to acknowledge in himself an element of the race pride that he had earlier critiqued as "a form of dementia that exists as a response to that form of white dementia that says blackness is nothing." Throughout the essay, then, Early sustains a complex interplay between personal reminiscence, personal confession, cultural interpretation, and cultural criticism, resulting in a fusion of perspectives that might be described as a culturally conscious "I."

Another version of the culturally conscious persona, moving back and forth between first- and third-person points of view, can be seen in Leslie Marmon Silko's "Yellow Woman and a Beauty of Spirit." But she uses a much less critical style and voice than Early. Silko opens her piece with four brief sentences that quickly establish her concern with the existential problem of difference, of "I" vis-à-vis "They," but in each case she uses a disarmingly plain style and matter-of-fact voice: "From the time I was a small child, I was aware that I was different. I looked different from my playmates. My two sisters looked different too. We didn't look quite like the other Laguna Pueblo children, but we didn't look quite white either." And she continues in the manner of a dispassionate informant, as she accounts for her different looks — her "yellow skin, brown hair, and green eyes" — by telling about the marriage between her Pueblo great-grandmother and her white great-grandfather. Only once does Silko openly speak of the anguish she felt at being mistreated because of her looks, when telling of how a white tourist about to "take photographs of us kids . . . motioned for me to step away from my classmates. I felt so embarrassed that I wanted to disappear." Otherwise, she maintains a calmly reportorial manner, like a cultural informant rather than a cultural critic, even when she explicitly brings up the issue of racism in an early passage that lays the groundwork for a sustained contrast between "traditional Pueblo societies" and "contemporary Western culture":

> Younger people, people my parents' age, seemed to look at the world in a more modern way. The modern way includes racism. My physical appearance seemed not to matter to the old-time people. They looked at the world very differently; a person's appearance and possessions did not matter nearly as much as a person's behavior.

Silko establishes that contrast so clearly and vividly in the first two segments of her piece that her cultural agenda is unmistakable — a celebration of "old-time" Pueblo spiritual, ethical, and social values versus a denigration of contemporary Western materialism. Once she has introduced the contrast, however, Silko rarely mentions contemporary Western culture again, focusing instead on distinctive aspects of old-time Pueblo culture, all of which are embodied in Kochininako, the Yellow Woman of Pueblo myth whom she celebrates in the conclusion of her essay. Thus Silko avoids a sustained attack on Western values and behavior, projecting herself as more tolerant by far than the white tourist who asked her to step away from her classmates.

Having lived for a time with Silko's piece and other essays engendered by the consciousness of difference and prejudice, I'm impressed, of course, by the profound change that such experience has wrought in the persona of the personal essayist, endowing a once indifferent "I" with an intense awareness of cultural conflict that has led during the past sixty years to an expanded range of perspectives and voices in the personal essay. I'm also fascinated by how such essayists have been shaped by the bitter experience of difference. But I'm not referring at this moment to whether they've chosen to come across as dispassionately as Dillard, Cofer, and Silko or as intensely as Baldwin, Walker, and Early, or to strike a balance of sorts like Rodriguez. Nor am I referring to whether they've chosen a single point of view, like Dillard and Cofer, or combined different perspectives and voices, like the others. I'm referring instead to the basic fact that they've evidently chosen to come across in ways they thought would make a difference in the reception of their work. So it might be said that having learned how one's visible appearance can make such a profound difference in the reception of their basic humanity, they have turned such prejudice to account by carefully crafting verbal appearances that might make a more profound and lasting difference in the reception of themselves and their work. No less protean than before, but endowed as never before with cultural consciousness.

ORWELL'S "A HANGING"
Politics and the First-Person Singular/Plural

This is an exhortation of sorts—to note the point of view in a personal essay. Such commonsense advice as to need no urging, were it not for the fact that the first-person singular is so conventional an aspect of the personal essay that it's taken for granted as the default point of view, and deviations from it are virtually ignored, as I discovered from the shock of realizing what I (and others) had missed by ignoring the split point of view in Orwell's "A Hanging." An essay as relevant for our own time as for Orwell's, given its haunting depiction of life and death in a far-flung colonial prison.

My story begins in a college English course some sixty years ago, when I first read "A Hanging"—so brief an essay and so transparent, it seemed, as to raise no problems of interpretation. How could there be any question of its central theme, its opposition to capital punishment, given the painfully detailed hanging it depicts and Orwell's memorable insight on the way to the gallows?

> It is curious, but till that moment I had never realized what
> it means to destroy a healthy, conscious man. When I saw the
> prisoner step aside to avoid the puddle I saw the mystery, the
> unspeakable wrongness, of cutting a life short when it is in full
> tide.

Reading that passage back then, I had no doubt of its import and neither did my instructor. Nor, in fact, have I ever had any question about its significance—"the unspeakable wrongness" speaks for itself. Speaks so clearly and forcefully that commentaries on the essay have invariably referred to that sentence as the essay's thematic statement. Indeed, twenty years after my first encounter with "A Hanging," Robert Scholes and I cited it in *Elements of the Essay* as "the persuasive point of the essay." Though we were concerned in that book with literary rather than expository forms of the essay, we were still influenced by the long-standing practice of interpreting an essay in terms of its author's thesis-like statements. And Orwell's essay looked like a perfect example, given its emblematic story and explicit thesis. Yet we paid hardly any attention to the narrator and his point of view, so compelled were we back then by Orwell's vividly detailed scenes and incidents—by the jail yard cells "like small animal cages," by the lashing of the prisoner's arms "tight to his sides," by the processional march to the gallows, by the prisoner's reiterated "crying out to his God," and the final image of the prisoner, "dangling with his toes pointed straight downward, very slowly revolving, as dead as a stone."

Given such disturbing images, it seemed perfectly reasonable to regard them as documentary evidence reflecting the evil of capital punishment and thus to regard the essay as being devoted to that theme. To think otherwise would have required an almost perverse refusal to recognize the obvious. Yet just a few years later, when I was teaching a graduate course on Orwell and a handful of other essayists, I was surprised and unsettled by aspects of "A Hanging" that I hadn't taken full stock of before—aspects that led me to perceive "the unspeakable wrongness" as just one part of the entire story and by no means the most important part. A counterintuitive reading, particularly given Orwell's well-known commitment to putting things as clearly and straightforwardly as possible.

My uneasiness was first aroused when I noticed that "A Hanging" involves a split point of view—first-person plural in most of the essay, except for the moment of insight and a few other spots in first-person singular, each no longer than a brief clause. Orwell's extensive use of the plural first-person was probably occasioned in part by his fidelity to the situation, since he viewed the hanging as part of an official group of jailers, magistrates, and the like. Even so, I was puzzled by the extent to which he portrayed himself as having been allied with the official group on the way to the gallows:

> We set out for the gallows. Two warders marched on either side of the prisoner. . . . The rest of us, magistrates and the like, followed behind. Suddenly, when we had gone ten yards, the procession stopped short without any order or warning. A dreadful thing had happened—a dog, come goodness knows whence had appeared in the yard. It came bounding among

us with a loud volley of barks, and leapt round us, wagging its whole body, wild with glee at finding so many human beings together. . . . For a moment it pranced round us, and then, before anyone could stop it, it had made a dash for the prisoner, and jumping up, tried to lick his feet. Everyone stood aghast, too taken aback even to grab at the dog. . . . It was several minutes before someone managed to catch the dog. Then we put my handkerchief through its collar and moved off once more, the dog still straining and whimpering.

Rereading this passage back then, I was struck by the fact that Orwell never uses the first-person singular, never separates himself from the group. More importantly, he portrays himself reacting exactly like the group, as aghast as his fellow officers at the behavior of the dog, as determined as they to restrain it. So he seems to be one with them in every sense—grammatically, physically, and psychologically.

It might be argued, I realize, that Orwell's alignment with the group is entirely reasonable at this point in the story, for it precedes his moment of insight. And it might also be said that by submerging himself so long within the group, his moment of insight is all the more dramatic for its sudden shift from plural- to first-person singular, as if Orwell himself had suddenly emerged from within the group. But just as surely it cannot be denied that by having set himself apart with that singular insight, it seems all the more notable that he suddenly shifts back to first-person plural and subsequently describes himself as having reacted just like his fellow officers, as if to suggest the unspoken power of the group to suppress individual thought. How else to account for the fact that at every crucial point in the remainder of the essay, he focuses on the unanimity of reactions within the group? When the prisoner is crying out to his god, and the hangman as well as everyone else is waiting for the command from the superintendent, Orwell takes note of their identical reactions:

We looked at the lashed, hooded man on the drop, and listened to his cries—each cry another second of life; the same thought was in all our minds: oh, kill him quickly, get it over, stop that abominable noise!

Shortly after the hanging has been completed, Orwell again goes out of his way to note the collective reactions of his group: "An enormous relief had come upon us now that the job was done. One felt an impulse to sing, to break into a run, to snigger. All at once everyone began chattering gaily." Then, after the head jailer, Francis, tells about a "refractory" prisoner who "clung to the bars of his cage" in hopes of avoiding the gallows, Orwell again takes note of the collective reaction in a way that explicitly equates his behavior with that of the group: "I found that I was laughing quite loudly. Everyone was laughing." And finally at the end of the piece, when the group is going off to drink together and a Burmese magistrate starts chuckling again at the jailer's story, Orwell again focuses on the collective reaction of his fellow officers and himself:

> We all began laughing again. At that moment Francis' anec-
> dote seemed extraordinarily funny. We all had a drink together,
> native and European alike, quite amicably. The dead man was a
> hundred yards away.

Such passages as these led me to see that Orwell was evidently interested not just in observing a hanging but also in observing the observers of the hanging. Indeed, from start to finish, he tracks their responses to the hanging as meticulously as the hanging itself. And as these passages suggest, Orwell seems intent on showing his reactions to have been virtually identical to those of the other observers, despite the moral insight that distinguishes him from them. So it seems all the more puzzling that commentators on Orwell have almost completely ignored these passages, as if his moment of insight had blinded them to everything else in the essay. But Orwell takes pains to highlight the inconsistency, by narrating his moment of insight immediately after expressing dismay with the antic dog, whose instinctively gentle nature is revealed by the fact that it first tries to lick the prisoner, then whines sympathetically in response to the prisoner's outcries, and finally retreats "into a corner of the yard" when it discovers the hanging body of the dead prisoner. Despite such innocent behavior, behavior that symbolically aligns it with his meditation on capital punishment, Orwell describes the creature near the end as "conscious of having misbehaved itself."

In the later paragraphs, Orwell's contradictory reactions and the bizarre reactions of his fellow observers become so prominent as to suggest that he may ultimately have been more intent on bearing witness to such behavior than he was in demonstrating "the unspeakable wrongness" of capital punishment. After all, the final scene of the essay painstakingly details the strange behavior of the several observers, Orwell included, while "the dead man" is only "a hundred yards away." How is one to account for such behavior? Why does Orwell focus on it? What does it suggest about the significance of the essay? Questions such as these have been on my mind since I first noticed these disturbing aspects of the piece, and they have led me to become increasingly dissatisfied with a literal reading of the essay, that is, with a reading that regards all of its narrative elements as evidence or support for the explicit statement against capital punishment.

I realize, of course, that the inappropriate reactions of Orwell and his fellow observers might well be considered a natural release of the extreme tension that follows so disturbing an event as a hanging, especially a hanging so vexed as this one appears to have been by the prolonged screaming of the prisoner. Such an explanation would surely account for the "impulse to sing, to break into a run, to snigger" that Orwell experienced upon leaving the gallows yard and walking through the central yard of the prison. As he says, "An enormous relief had come upon us now that the job was done." But this explanation alone doesn't seem adequate to explain the raucous laughter that Orwell chooses to describe in the final scene of the essay, especially given the fact that the outburst doesn't take place until Francis has completed his story of the "refractory" prisoner—a story that he tells the superintendent in order to demonstrate by contrast the "utmost satisfactoriness" of the hanging that has just taken place:

> "One man, I recall, clung to the bars of hiss cage when we went to take him out. You will scarcely credit, sir, that it took six warders to dislodge him, three pulling at each leg. We reasoned with him. 'My dear fellow,' we said, 'think of all the pain and trouble you are causing us!' But no, he would not listen! Ach, he wass very troublesome!" I found that I was laughing quite loudly. Everyone was laughing. Even the superintendent grinned in a tolerant way.

In this case, the laughter appears to have been aroused primarily by the grotesque image that Francis recalls in the first half of his story and by the grotesque dialogue that he reports in the second half. As a result, the already charged situation is suddenly suffused with something very much like the aura of black humor, provoked by Francis's obsequiously self-serving tale. The final paroxysm of laughter is also the by-product of Francis's story: "'Pulling at his legs!' exclaimed a Burmese magistrate suddenly, and burst into a loud chuckling. We all began laughing again. At that moment Francis' anecdote seemed extraordinarily funny." Only under such bizarre circumstances (eerily prescient of Abu Ghraib) would anyone possibly consider Francis's anecdote to be "extraordinarily funny," as Orwell makes clear by the adverbial phrase "at that moment." In that spare phrase, he tacitly distances himself from his earlier behavior, as if to register a belated sense of guilt for his complicity in the raucous laughter. Concluding as it does on this disturbing note, the essay might well be seen as a full-scale revelation of the strange behavior that the hanging provokes in everyone who is party to it, as if to suggest that everyone is undone by it.

But it's also important to note that this particular hanging itself has been a very strange affair, as one can see by focusing on Orwell's narrative technique, which is notable at the start for its unusually detailed description of the warders readying the prisoner for the gallows—more detail than is strictly necessary. But the detail serves to reveal that the hanging was evidently carried out in accordance with something very much like a military protocol:

> Six tall Indian warders were guarding him and getting him ready for the gallows. Two of them stood by with rifles and fixed bayonets, while the others handcuffed him, passed a chain through his handcuffs and fixed it to their belts, and lashed his arms tight to his sides. They crowded very close to him, with their hands always on him in a careful, caressing grip, as though all the while feeling him to make sure he was there.

Given Orwell's previous description of the prisoner as "a puny wisp of a man," such an elaborate method of guarding and pinioning him must have been dictated by a set of regulations, rather than by some immediate necessity to take precautions against his escape. After tracking down a colonial Burmese jail manual of the period, I found just such a rule:

Prior to his removal from the cell, the prisoner shall be dressed in a cotton gown long enough to reach his ankles, and his arms shall be securely pinioned behind his back.

Additional evidence of regulated procedure comes immediately after the pinioning, when Orwell notes that "eight o'clock struck," and then reports a conversation in which the superintendent tells the head jailer that "The man ought to have been dead by this time. . . . The prisoners can't get their breakfast till this job's over." A haunting revelation that prison regulations must have called for a specifically timed sequence of events—that is, a hanging to be completed by or shortly before eight o'clock, and breakfast to be served only after the hanging had been completed. Or as the Burmese manual puts it:

The early morning shall be selected as the time for execution. The prisoners in the jail shall not be made to attend, and shall, as a rule, be kept in their sleeping-wards until the execution has taken place.

The most striking evidence of official procedure can be seen in Orwell's description of the "procession" to the gallows. Though it was only forty yards away from the jail yard, the prisoner, according to Orwell, was accompanied there by an elaborate escort:

Two warders marched on either side of the prisoner, their rifles at the slope; two others marched close against him, gripping him by arm and shoulder, as though at once pushing and supporting him. The rest of us, magistrates and the like, followed behind.

Such a formal procession over so short a distance, it's hardly surprising that when the dog interrupts the procession and a jailer attempts "to stone the dog away," Orwell notes that the prisoner "looked on incuriously, as though this was another formality of the hanging." Formality, indeed, is what Orwell seems to emphasize in his description of the hanging—formality so elaborately detailed and so solemnly carried out as to constitute a prescribed ritual.

But from the point at which the dog interrupts the procession, every important aspect of the ritual appears to be violated. For example, once the dog has been caught and Orwell's "handkerchief" has been put "through its collar," the dog itself is included in the procession, "still straining and whimpering." And once this irregular procession has reached the gallows and the noose has been placed on the prisoner's neck, he begins "crying out . . . over and over again . . . on and on," for so long a period of time that the hangman is transfixed, "holding the lever," rather than pulling it "quickly," as stipulated by the manual. The hangman's delay and the prisoner's continued screaming cause the Indian warders to turn "gray like bad coffee" and their bayonets to begin "wavering," while the superintendent is reduced to "poking the ground with his stick." In fact, the irregularities continue, even after the superintendent has commanded the hangman to pull the lever, and the prisoner has suddenly dropped through the trap door of the gallows, for just then Orwell inadvertently lets go of the dog, and "it gallop[s] immediately to the back of the gallows," as if to conduct its own inspection of the prisoner before any of the official party. So many deviations from official procedure that it's absurd of Francis to claim that "all has passed off with the utmost satisfactoriness," that "it was all finished—flick! like that." Actually, an adherence to procedure is reclaimed only after the superintendent pokes the prisoner's dead body and notes the time as "eight minutes past eight," at which point Orwell reports that "the warders unfixed bayonets and marched away."

As these passages suggest, Orwell seems to be preoccupied with both the protocol for a hanging and the deviations from protocol that took place during this particular execution. Indeed, this preoccupation so pervades the essay that it might well be considered a more compelling center of interest than the encapsulated commentary against capital punishment. The essay is dominated by a consciousness of protocol because everyone involved in the hanging (except for the prisoner and the dog) is intensely devoted to it. So extreme is their devotion that they endow it with the significance of a moral imperative, as exemplified by the superintendent in his opening conversation with Francis: "'For God's sake hurry up, Francis,' he said irritably. 'The man ought to have been dead by this time.'" Given such an imperative, such a moral "ought," any and all deviations from protocol call forth intense reactions, comparable to what might be provoked by the breaking of a taboo. So it is that when the dog interrupts the procession, Orwell speaks of its interruption as being "a dreadful thing" and notes that "everyone stood aghast, too taken aback even to grab at the dog." So too the superintendent immediately reacts to the dog by calling it "that bloody brute." And so it is that Orwell regards the dog's timorous behavior at the end as a sign that it was "conscious of having misbehaved itself."

This intense commitment to protocol also helps explain one of the most disturbing and vexing moments in the piece, when Orwell reports how he and his fellow observers reacted to the reiterated cries of the prisoner:

> We looked at the lashed, hooded man on the drop, and listened to his cries — each cry another second of life; the same thought was in all our minds: oh, kill him quickly, get it over, stop that abominable noise.

Initially, this passage seems to convey a compassionate reaction on the part of Orwell and his fellow witnesses, "oh, kill him quickly," as if they wish for the prisoner to be put out of his misery. But as the passage unfolds, it reveals that they have become so impatient with the delay, "get it over," and then so offended by the prisoner's cries that Orwell refers to the crying as "that abominable noise." Orwell's reaction at this point might well seem puzzling, given that it comes only moments after his reflection on the "unspeakable wrongness of cutting a life short." But when his reaction is seen within the context of the entire piece, it serves as an epitome of the powerful, almost tyrannical, influence that protocol exerts over everyone involved in the incident.

Orwell's reaction at this moment also reveals the warrant for such a strict adherence to protocol. Like any ritual, the protocol for a hanging was intended to endow the activity with the dignity of a sacred event, or as England's Capital Punishment Amendment Act of 1868 put it, "the rules and regulations to be observed on the execution of death in every prison" are intended as a means "of giving greater solemnity to the same." An aura of "greater solemnity" was surely needed back then, given the raucous crowds that once attended public hangings. But just as surely it must have helped prison officials to conduct hangings without feeling an intolerable sense of guilt. By rigorously formalizing all the elements of a hanging, the protocol assured that the process could be carried out swiftly, without any time for uncomfortable thoughts, such as Orwell's, to arise in the minds of the official participants. In 1953, for example, the Royal Commission on Capital Punishment reported that in England and Scotland, an average of less than one minute elapsed between opening the prisoner's cell and pulling the drop cord on the gallows, the variation in time depending largely on the distance between the cell and the gallows. By contrast, it appears that at least eight minutes elapsed before completion of the hanging reported by Orwell—plenty of time for him to have had the disturbing thoughts that came to mind after the dog had interrupted the procession, and time as well for the superintendent to suffer the temporary paralysis of intent that he experienced once the prisoner started crying out to his god. Thus the screaming of the prisoner would have been "abominable" to Orwell and his fellow witnesses not only because it shattered the formality and speedy conclusion of the ritual but also because it suddenly made them aware of the prisoner's anguish, his basic humanity, and thus deprived them of the psychological distancing they might otherwise have gained from the ritual.

Considered in this context, the grotesque behavior of the final scene becomes all the more intelligible, for it dramatically reveals the hysterical reactions that ensue when protocol is violated. In his own bizarre way, Francis confirms this truth when he tells the story of the "very troublesome" prisoner who did not realize "all the pain and trouble" he was causing the officials by his "refractory" behavior. Coincidentally, Francis's garrulous storytelling also reveals that the superintendent is evidently new to the business of hanging, for he prefaces each of his stories by statements that contrast the hanging just completed with other more disturbing executions—"It iss not always so" and "ach, sir, it is worse when they become refractory"—as if to imply that the superintendent himself has no basis on which to judge the experience he has just been through. And the superintendent's reaction reinforces this implication, when he says "Wriggling about, eh? That's bad."

So, it's no exaggeration to say that from start to finish, Orwell's essay bears witness to a hanging that departs from protocol for a variety of reasons—an intruding dog, a crying prisoner, an incompetent hangman, an inexperienced superintendent, and a garrulous head jailer. Varied as those causes are, they conspire to produce a final scene that is remarkably unified not only by its raucous laughter, but also by its conviviality among a culturally disparate group of individuals who might otherwise have nothing to do with each other. Orwell, for example, finds himself approached by a Eurasian boy, who offers him a cigarette and with "a knowing smile" tells how the prisoner "pissed on the floor of his cell" when he learned that his appeal had been dismissed. Francis tells his gallows stories to the superintendent and the rest of the laughing group. The superintendent in turn invites everyone to "come out and have a drink. . . . We could do with it." On the way out, the Burmese magistrate's outburst of laughter causes everyone to begin "laughing." And then everyone has "a drink together, native and European alike, quite amicably," while the dead man is only "a hundred yards away."

Except for the stark image of the prisoner's body, the sociable revelries that transpire in this final scene might well befit the celebratory conclusion of a comedy—a radical departure, to say the least, from the solemn protocol of a hanging. Such camaraderie would have been considered all the more remarkable by Orwell's English readers in 1931, given the widely publicized colonial tensions and convulsions that had prevailed in Burma throughout the twenties. Orwell documented those tensions five years later in the vivid images of Burmese-colonial conflict that appear at the outset of "Shooting an Elephant." But for the purposes of this earlier piece, it was sufficient for him just to allude to those tensions in order to suggest how far this hanging had deviated from protocol, and how drastically that deviation had influenced the behavior of everyone connected with it. So, too, he evidently considered it sufficient to mention his laughter just once in order to suggest how far his own behavior had strayed from his earlier meditation on capital punishment.

All in all, this final scene epitomizes the complex psychological happenings that Orwell has depicted throughout this unusual hanging—a hanging that he portrays as having been disturbing both because it led him to see the "unspeakable wrongness" of capital punishment and because it compelled him to recognize the unspeakably complex way in which legalized regulations, public rituals, and social communities conspire to suppress such a painfully moral consciousness as his own. By showing the powerful influence of those forces upon everyone involved in the hanging, especially himself, and by showing how those competing influences put him at odds with his own humane values, he seems to be implying at last that capital punishment cannot be dismissed simply by a sweeping moral indictment of it.

As this commentary suggests, "A Hanging" embodies a much more complex view of capital punishment than one might suppose from Orwell's forthright statement against it. This complexity, as I have tried to show, results from the fact that Orwell's statement is set within a narrative framework, which is itself complicated by Orwell's split point of view in narrating the hanging and by his correspondingly ambiguous depiction of himself, as well as by the elaborate protocol for a hanging and by the bizarre events that violate it. So, in discussing the essay, I have not been free just to cite the statement against capital punishment and touch on a few of the grimmest moments in the hanging, as do most studies of Orwell that comment on the piece. Instead, it has been necessary to examine the essay's narrative form, its point of view, plot, dialogue, and descriptive detail, trying to account for problematic material from every section of it. To complicate matters further, Orwell does not explicitly discuss the importance of protocol, nor does he explain all the regulations that it involves, as he might in an article on hanging. He shows it in action (and in abeyance), rather than telling about it in so many words, necessitating a reconstruction of the protocol from the text itself and from regulations set forth in colonial Burmese documents of the period, in order to demonstrate how deeply embedded it is in the essay. The form of "A Hanging," in other words, is as meaningful as that of a short story or a poem. It works by implication. Thus, it cannot properly be understood by a literal interpretation; it requires a detailed literary explication.

It might be argued that because of its split point of view, "A Hanging" is an unrepresentative personal essay and, therefore, that the interpretative problems it raises are atypical. But even an essay completely in first-person singular, such as "Shooting an Elephant," which contains an extended meditation on "the hollowness, the futility of the white man's dominion in the East," as well as a straightforward statement of theme — "that when the white man turns tyrant it is his own freedom that he destroys" — even such a clearly pointed essay turns out to be more complex than it seems, for its

apparently single point of view incorporates the distinctly different perceptions of a present and past consciousness, of a self remembering and a remembered self, that are clearly not one and the
same. Most narrative essays involve such a layering or interplay of
present and past perception, and the layering is often as significant
as the story itself, particularly in essays that center on political or
social issues. For an altered consciousness or a coming to consciousness is often at the heart of the matter. In "Shooting an Elephant,"
Orwell highlights the difference right off by giving a detailed portrait of his youthful state of mind at the time of the incident that he
subsequently narrates. In "A Hanging," it becomes manifest near
the end when Orwell refers to "that moment" at which "Francis'
anecdote seemed extraordinarily funny," as if to make clear that he
no longer thinks so, and thereby implicitly renders judgment upon
himself for having thought so back then, unnerved as he was both
by the prisoner's anguish and by the boisterous camaraderie of his
fellow officers.

In citing these two cases, I don't mean to minimize the significance of propositional statements that appear to speak for the
whole of a personal or political essay. But I do mean to suggest
that such essays are generally more complex than they have usually
been taken to be, because they often embody a split point of view,
a double perspective, and because they often involve tensions between the consciousness of an individual and the pressures of a
group. Accordingly, such essays are as likely to enact their meaning as to assert it openly, and even the ideas they openly assert exist
in such a formally intricate web as not to be susceptible of simple
extraction. As Hoagland has pointedly observed, "A personal essay
is like the human voice talking, its order the mind's natural flow,
instead of a systematized outline of ideas. . . . Essays don't usually
boil down to a summary, as articles do." So, it's risky to extract even
the most rhetorically or stylistically prominent passages and read
them literally as containing the point of the piece. At the least, one
may be in danger of simplification, at the worst of "unspeakable
wrongness."

IV

*Personae
and Personal
Experience*

ILLNESS AND "I"

Malady in the Personal Essay

T wenty-five years ago on an evening in late February, Kate and I had just finished a dinner of stir-fried pork, hot and sour bok choy, steamed rice, and fresh daikon radishes, so it hardly surprised me that I was burping up the taste of those radishes as she cleared the table and I prepared to take out the garbage. I had, after all, had more than my share of them. Six months later, I came to see those radishy burpings as the harbinger of a radically new kind of life for both of us, since they were, as it turns out, the first signs of a heart attack. A mild attack followed by another four days later, without benefit of daikon, since I was then in the local hospital, followed by an ambulance ride to the nearby university hospital's cardiac care unit, where the head cardiologist greeted me with a plumb bob and a yardstick, which he would use, he said, to determine the exact location of my heart, followed by an angiogram two days later to discover the exact amount of blockage in my coronary arteries—some crown!—followed by eleven days on intravenous blood thinners, nitroglycerin, sedatives, and other fluids to calm a restive heart and quell a type-A mentality before the crowning insult of a triple bypass. Otherwise known by the flamboyant misnomer of "open heart surgery."

Six months later, when I was teaching again and writing again and beginning to see a connection between those daikon radishes and the Zen of my new existence, I was often so moved by the rush of my recollections that I might easily have written a lengthy and vividly detailed personal essay about my heart attack and its surgical and psychological aftermath. But who would have published a piece detailing the whole gory process—the breast bone sawed completely in half, the ribs pulled all the way back, the heart temporarily stilled, the lungs temporarily shut down, the heart-lung machine set into motion, a mammary artery harvested from one side of the chest and a vein harvested from the entire length of one leg to serve as bypasses around the blocked coronary arteries, and then the whole contraption wired and sewn back together again, with drainage tubes coming out of the chest, a breathing tube coming out of the mouth, intravenous tubes coming out of the arms, and God knows what else? And who would have wanted to read about the tears coming out of my eyes some ten hours later at the first faint sounds of Kate's voice; or about the pain working its way through my chest at the first faint return of neural sensations; or about the fear suddenly coming to mind that one of the bypasses might fail or the whole heart itself go wild, if not right then, then sometime later, in the garden, in bed, in love, on the stool, in class; or about my first faint awareness that the bypass wasn't really a cure or a permanent repair but just a temporary holding action against the inexorable working of the disease; or about my first hazy realization that in body and psyche I wasn't at all like I had been just a few days before and that for better or worse I would never be the same again? And how would I have managed to produce an exactingly detailed, artfully crafted, and richly significant account of my personal experience, while also confining it to the length of a publishable essay?

Questions such as those might have passed through my mind back then, if I had even faintly entertained the possibility of writing an essay about the experience. But the thought of doing so never really crossed my mind. There were, after all, so few essayistic precedents for a personal account of physical or mental affliction, and those by such eminent writers—Didion on her migraines, Fitzgerald on his crackup—that the idea of writing something about my heart attack would have seemed ludicrous to me. Now, just twenty-five years later, so many personal essays have appeared about so many physical and psychological afflictions—from anorexia, atrial fibrillation, breast cancer, and multiple sclerosis to prostate cancer, paraplegia, poliomyelitis, and unipolar depression—that a piece about coronary artery disease could surely find its way into print, except perhaps for the fact that essayists have already taken stock of it in plentiful detail.

Nancy Mairs pioneered this contemporary phenomenon in *Plaintext*, a collection of essays published in 1986, focusing on her struggles with multiple sclerosis, chronic depression, and agoraphobia. And Mairs's insistence on speaking out about her situation as an emblem of the manifold contradictions in a woman's life clearly suggests that personal essays about malady should be seen at least in part as an outgrowth of contemporary feminism. Since then, however, the subject of malady has been taken up by men and women alike, often without any particular ax to grind beyond the story of their distinctive experiences. Malady, in fact, has now become such a hot topic of personal essays that other book-length collections have been devoted to it. Indeed, the subject has now been so widely valorized that pieces about malady have regularly made their way into recent editions of *The Best American Essays*.

Such pieces compel attention not only because of their visceral subject matter, but also because they constitute a distinctly new kind of personal essay. An essay so intensely personal both in its subject matter and in its author's presence that it violates some of the most long-standing conventions of the personal essay. How is it possible, one might ask, for a personal essay to become too personal? A personal slant, after all, is by definition its distinguishing feature. But contemporary essays about malady stand out by focusing on subjects previously considered so intimate as to be completely off-limits—such as Harold Brodkey's AIDS and AIDS-induced pneumonia, Anatole Broyard's prostate cancer, Andre Dubus's automobile accident and ensuing paraplegia, Stanley Elkin's fortnight of madness brought on by an excess of Prednisone, Patricia Foster's anorexia, Lucy Grealy's jaw cancer and facial reconstruction, Judith Hooper's lumpectomy and ensuing chemotherapy, Nancy Mairs's attempted suicides, Adalaide Morris's hysterectomy, and Joyce Winer's apparent infertility and subsequent pregnancy. In their forthright discussion of private matters, these essayists stand out by "uttering" what Mairs refers to as "the unspeakable," transgressing "the boundaries of polite—that is, conventional—discourse."

In their preoccupation with the circumstantial details and existential realities of personal affliction, such essays constitute a distinctly new subgenre that is not specific to either gender but is instead a manifestation, at least in part, of the contemporary phenomenon that Broyard called "a literature of illness" and Mairs has referred to as "the literature of personal disaster" in *Voice Lessons*. This new personal genre might also be thought to include the essay-like stories and case histories of Drs. Richard Selzer and Oliver Sacks. But it's one thing to write about illness from the specialized perspective of a doctor and quite another to write about it from the firsthand experience of having suffered through an affliction one-self. Though Mairs may be correct in asserting that "more women than men seem attracted to" such literature, I'm not sure I'd agree with her claim that "the works of women tend to be more intimate and immediate than those of men," not at least in the case of the essay. Men and women who write about their maladies seem to me to be equally vivid and intimate in narrating their experiences. They don't just allude to the unspeakable, nor do they mention it only in passing, as Montaigne does his kidney stone. They dwell upon it at length, whether it happens to be a man such as Elkins telling about an episode of urinary incompetence during his Prednisone-induced period of madness or a woman such as Winer remembering an episode of bloodstained urine during the early stage of her pregnancy. And as if to relive the particularities of their malady as viscerally as possible, the authors of such pieces often narrate their personal accounts in graphic and clinical detail.

Sometimes, like Elkin, they go so far as to offer a complete run-down of all their other serious maladies from childhood on—"I spent first grade in a hospital room in Chicago, did a year in bed in the Michael Reese Hospital for a deep strep throat in the pre-penicillin dark ages. . . . In 1985 I had quintuple heart bypass surgery, three years later they went back in and gave me a quadruple. That same year I had an endartectomy and a second heart attack." Sometimes, like Winer, they offer a more highly focused case history—"Like many women born after 1945, I remained in charge of my body during my twenties and thirties. Which means that during that time I was either on the pill, or the coil, or the diaphragm. . . . I got my period regularly. I never got cramps or *mittelschmerttz* or PMS." Sometimes, like Elkin, they tell their stories in past tense, in the manner of a continuous narrative, or case history—"I'm told by Bernie that just after I was put into my hospital bed (the sides of which rise like a crib's) I had to use the plastic urinal; that I couldn't get my penis into it; that the nurse bent over and did it for me; and that when she did I touched her breasts." Sometimes, like Winer, they write their accounts in present tense, in the style of a log or journal, consisting of several discrete entries—"I have to pee a lot. Late on a Saturday afternoon at the end of my third month, I'm hefting a new gallon jug of milk onto the top shelf of the refrigerator when I feel the small burst, the trickle soaking my underpants. In the bathroom, I sit and look down between my thighs at the blood leaking into the toilet."

Whatever narrative technique (or combination of techniques) they use, such vivid detailing of experience usually leads to the re-animation of intense feeling about it — "All the wanting, all the wait-ing, and my body is once again asserting itself, rejecting my efforts in a steady bright red stream. I scream. I hate my body. I want to grab it and shake it into submission. I want to punish it by lashing myself upside down to the wall until the bleeding stops." And the feeling, in turn, usually leads to reflection upon the experience — "Once I could occupy myself with idle, inconsequential musings about the reason for my infertility while I lay plans to overcome it. But no matter what the cause, I can no longer blame the consequences of my infertility on either dumb luck or the inexorable movement of some divine plan." These essayists spiral incessantly around the most private aspects of their affliction, reliving it, reflecting upon it, coming to terms with it in one way or another — "This wasn't any amazing grace that had happened to me. It wasn't a case of I once was lost but now I'm found, was blind but now I see. It would be a month or more before I satisfactorily processed information again . . . it sometimes took me a day to write two letters, trying to explain myself, what had happened to me."

Hardly the kind of experience one would expect to hear about from the genteel American essayists who were writing at the begin-ning of the twentieth century, or from their English counterparts. "Ladies and gentlemen talk together," as Virginia Woolf said in her attempt to evoke the drawing room ambience that once suffused the personal essay, "and some things, of course, are not said." So, in her essay "On Being Ill," one of the few pieces of the time to discuss such a topic, Woolf mentions several maladies that deserve a place in literature — influenza, pneumonia, typhoid, and toothache — but she never hints at any specific personal experience that might have given rise to her reflections on illness. Even before that era of Edwardian and post-Edwardian proprieties, personal essayists had long abided by an elaborate set of courtesies — "conspiracies of silence," as Mairs calls them — about what could and could not be said. Were it not for those courtesies and conspiracies, Montaigne would "very gladly have portrayed" himself "entire and wholly naked." Instead, he evidently felt constrained to be only as intimate about his private life "as respect for the public" would allow. Even in his lengthy essay "On Some Verses of Virgil," in which he promises to give a candid discussion of "the sexual act," Montaigne offers only scattered allusions to his own sexual activities and his declining sexual powers.

As if to echo that sense of restraint—and inadvertently reveal its sexist premises—E. B. White, in a letter to his biographer Scott Elledge (February 16, 1964), described the essayist as someone "who must take his trousers off without showing his genitals." So, although White reportedly suffered from recurring bouts of depression, hypochondria, and other psychological as well as physical afflictions, he never dwelt upon them in his essays, limiting himself instead to self-deprecating remarks about his unsteady moods. In fact, even when he was evidently sick in bed, as he makes clear at the beginning of "Bedfellows," White chose to ignore the illness almost completely, except for humorous recollections of his dead dachshund Fred, who "always attended the sick, climbing right into the bed with the patient like some lecherous old physician, and making a bad situation worse." Or if he identified the illness and discussed it at all, as in "The Summer Catarrh," he chose to make it an occasion for humor, comparing himself in that essay to Daniel Webster, who also suffered from catarrh, otherwise known today as hay fever.

But why all this fuss about the content of a personal essay? Subject matter restrictions, after all, are literary conventions that usually reflect the exigencies of time and place, class and culture, especially in an occasional form of writing such as the essay. So, not surprisingly, the drastically altered cultural, social, and political circumstances of later twentieth-century life have, in turn, produced a considerably greater latitude in the content of the personal essay. And that, it would seem, is all one need say about the matter. Yet the latitude in subject matter reflects a significant change in the motives that essayists bring to their writing. These changes can be seen by noting how essayists account for writing so intimately about themselves. To some extent, especially in the case of feminists, essays about malady have developed out of a self-conscious intention to go against the grain of the traditional courtesies. Mairs, for example, who is the most outspoken proponent of the unspeakable, repeatedly declares her refusal to be silenced by traditional rules of conduct and repeatedly explains that her cultural defiance is engendered by a desire to undo the repressive effects of those rules—"to undermine their power to constrict my life and the lives of any others whose voices had been choked off by social taboos." In one respect, then, Mairs's persistence in writing about her physical and mental afflictions is a political as well as personal activity.

But beyond the countercultural motive that energizes all her writing, Mairs discusses her essays as if they were a mode of therapy. To begin with, the therapy is directed toward herself—"In writing about my experience, I am, first of all trying to make sense of it and to make it bearable for myself." And self-oriented therapy evidently deals with several different problems arising from severe maladies. Writing about such experience not only "counteracts disorientation and disintegration," but it "also produces the impression—generally quite groundless—of control, which may save one's sanity even though it can't save one's own or anyone else's life," and it serves "to reconnect myself . . . to the human community." Mairs's intense concern with writing as a mode of overcoming the sense of alienation and isolation produced by severe illness leads her, in turn, to a reciprocal interest in the psychic well-being of her readers—"But I am also trying to draw you into it, to carry you along through it, so that whatever extraordinary circumstances you one day meet—and you will, because all creatures do—you will have, in some way, 'been there' before." Thus she sees her essays as offering others "companionship in a common venture" and thereby a form of "comfort." Occasionally, she also claims to have an "esthetic drive: to transmute dross—my own hastening physical deterioration; my husband's wretched, retching progress through chemotherapy—into lapidary reality." Occasionally, too, she writes about the importance of transcending one's "ordeals," in order "to speak generally, and generously, of the human condition." But Mairs gives much less space to artistic and literary declarations than to the therapeutic dimension of her intimate self-disclosures. For Mairs, then, the essayist writing about malady casts herself in the role of a defiantly self-revealing presence, in order to provide therapy both for herself and her readers—a role that tends to put the reader in the position of being someone like a fellow-sufferer, therapist, trusted friend, or close relative, willing to hear all without embarrassment or judgment.

Anatole Broyard also seems to take a therapeutic view in his essay "Toward a Literature of Illness." Like Mairs, he begins by focusing on therapy for himself — "my first instinct was to try to bring it under control by turning it into narrative. . . . Just as a novelist turns his anxiety into a story in order to be able to control it, so a sick person can make a story, a narrative, out of his illness as a way of trying to detoxify it." And like Mairs, he then perceives his "extraordinary experience" as a means of providing guidance for others — "Like a convert who's had a vision, I wanted to preach it, to tell people what a serious illness is like, the unprecedented ideas and fantasies it puts into your head, the unexpected qualms and quirks it introduced into your body." But Broyard ultimately pushes toward a view of writing about malady that is far more existential than therapeutic — "it seems to me that every seriously ill person needs to develop a style for his illness. I think that only by insisting on your style can you keep from falling out of love with yourself as the illness attempts to diminish you. Sometimes your vanity is the only thing that's keeping you alive, and your style is the instrument of your vanity." So, at last, Broyard concludes by noting that "the best reason in the world" for writing about his illness is "to make sure I'll be alive when I die."

Given such distinctive essayistic stances as Mairs's and Broyard's, I decided to talk with my colleague Patricia Foster, to see if she might shed some additional light on writing about malady from her experience as both an author and an editor of such essays. When I asked what had led her to write about such intimate aspects of her own personal life, she immediately responded by saying that it was "an act of salvation," "a way of saving my life." Such phrases led me to suggest that it sounded as if the self-exposure of such writing was for her, as for Mairs, primarily a form of therapy. "No, it's not just therapeutic," she replied, "because you have to use style, voice, artifice, in writing about such aspects of your experience — and doing so transforms the self in ways that might never take place in therapy." Though I heard a clear-cut literary orientation in those remarks, I still couldn't help sensing a therapeutic motive in them as well — admittedly achieved by aesthetic rather than psychological means, but a beneficial transformation of the self just the same. "Going to the hot spots, to the raw places," she then explained, "is most important for me, because it's a way of getting as close as one can to the most intimate and interior dimensions of the self. And I want to get there partly to articulate the kinds of anguish that exist for any human being. But as a fiction writer, I also can't help thinking of those intimate, delicate moments in novels that are the most fascinating and compelling because they are the most revealing of the interior self, of the human psyche. If we can have such moments in fiction—and also, by the way, in memoir—why shouldn't we assume that the same kind of material can be dealt with in the personal essay, and just as artistically?" According to Foster, then, the heightened intimacy of writing about personal malady derives its validity from a commitment to the intimacy and interiority that have long existed in fictionalized and extended autobiographical narrative.

Hearing such a deliberate intent to get "as close as one can to the most intimate and interior dimensions of the self," I couldn't help thinking of how differently essayists defined the personal element at the beginning of the twentieth century. Most of them, like Woolf, were celebrating the "personality" of the essayist, intoning that word like a mantra, as if it were the be-all and end-all of the essay. Thus in an omnibus review for the *North American Review*, Louise Collier Willcox celebrated the English essayist Arthur Benson, because his work embodied the presence "of a gentle, leisurely scholar, surrounded by the best culture of his day, dwelling in one of the most beautiful cities of the world, looking out upon life from his vine-draped college windows upon the velvety college courts, and dedicating his chief thoughts to the enlargement of spirit which grows out of sympathy and truth." Given such an elitist and sexist conception of the essayist and the essay, it's hardly conceivable that essayists of that period would even have imagined the possibility of writing about their personal maladies.

In the years since then, of course, personal essayists have come out of their ivory towers, their book-lined studies and their stuffy drawing rooms, increasingly confronting the more troubled circumstances of twentieth-century life. But through most of the twentieth century, personal essayists generally aimed to project themselves as engaging and stimulating companions, not wanting to burden readers with any of their personal afflictions. And readers, in turn, generally expected essayists to provide them such companionship. So, not surprisingly, when Joan Didion's *The White*

Album appeared in 1979, opening with a detailed psychiatric report of Didion's physical and mental condition in 1968, even reviewers familiar with her "inside-of-the-stomach stuff" were shocked by the intimacy of her self-exposure. "The candor frequently stuns," as Michiko Kakutani put it in a *New York Times* interview-based portrait of her in 1979. "She tells us how she went blind for six weeks from a condition diagnosed as multiple sclerosis (the disease has been in remission for the past seven years), and how, in the summer of 1968, she checked into the psychiatric clinic at St. John's Hospital in Santa Monica. She even tells us the doctor's diagnosis." The world of essayists and readers was evidently not altogether ready even then for the work of someone who believes that "if you want to write about yourself, you have to give them something."

Essays about malady now appear widely in magazines ranging from the *Iowa Review*, the *Kenyon Review*, and the *Seattle Review* to *Harper's*, *Lear's*, and the *New Yorker*. And they need to be reckoned with, like them or not, because they clearly embody a radical transformation of the essayist's persona and the essayist's tacit relationship to the reader, and because they incorporate such a radically new kind of subject matter in the personal essay. I'm tempted to speculate about why personal essayists suddenly took up writing about such experiences in the late 1980s — the AIDS pandemic, the breast cancer epidemic, the widespread incidence of heart disease, and the increased public awareness of these and other severely crippling or fatal afflictions. Severe maladies, it seems, have become such a widespread experience of our time that few people have been untouched by them either personally or at close hand. No one is an island entire of itself. Everyone is a piece of the continent, a part of the main. And few people have been untouched by the extraordinary medical procedures that have been developed for the diagnosis, treatment, and prevention of such afflictions — angiograms, bone marrow transplants, CAT-scans, coronary artery bypasses, magnetic resonance imaging, mammograms, prostate specific antigens, Tamoxifen therapy. Severe afflictions are now so familiar a part of everyone's personal experience that their intimate subject matter is no longer so intimate as to be taboo. Nowadays, even our most public — and hitherto private — figures publicly announce their afflictions. So, if our sports heroes and our movie idols can tell us about being afflicted with AIDS, and our ex-presidents can tell us about their Alzheimer's disease, and their wives can tell us about their breast cancer, why can't personal essayists also write about such experiences? Nothing, any longer, is too personal for the personal essay.

But beyond the culturally liberating circumstances of our time, I'm still concerned with the question of what has driven essayists to write about such experience and the equally important matter of how to define or name the new kind of essay that embodies such experience. For insight into these questions, I find myself drawn back again to Virginia Woolf's essay "On Being Ill," which begins with a hauntingly detailed evocation of the radical transformations brought about by illness—"how tremendous the spiritual change that it brings, how astonishing, when the lights of health go down, the undiscovered countries that are then disclosed, what wastes and deserts of the soul a slight attack of influenza brings to view, what precipices and lawns sprinkled with bright flowers a little rise of temperature reveals, what ancient and obdurate oaks are uprooted in us by the act of sickness." Considering "how common" such experience is, Woolf finds it "strange indeed that illness has not taken its place with love and battle and jealousy among the prime themes of literature."

Though Woolf was evidently thinking only about fiction, poetry, and drama in her reference to literature, her remarks have a special relevance to the issues at hand, particularly when she seeks to account for the "strange" oversight of illness—"literature does its best to maintain that its concern is with the mind, that the body is a sheet of plain glass through which the soul looks straight and clear, and, save for one or two passions such as desire and greed, is null, and negligible and non-existent." The essay, it seems to me, has long sought to maintain just such a posture — "that its concern is with the mind." Montaigne, for example, repeatedly proclaimed in one form or another that "It is my thoughts that I portray." And four hundred years later one can hear the echo of Montaigne in the numerous essayists who speak of their work in similar terms, as "mind speaking to mind," as "thought itself in orbit," as "a stroll through someone's mazy mind." By virtue of this widely and persistently held conviction, essayists, I think, have long contributed to the mind-body split that Woolf sought to overcome in her reflections on illness—"The creature within can only gaze through the pane—smudged or rosy; it cannot separate off from the body like the sheath of a knife or the pod of a pea for a single instant; it must go through the whole unending procession of changes, heat and cold, comfort and discomfort, hunger and satisfaction, health and illness, until there comes the inevitable catastrophe; the body smashes itself to smithereens, and the soul (it is said) escapes. But of all this daily drama of the body there is no record. People write always of the doings of the mind; the thoughts that come into it."

So, at last, it seems that in choosing to write of their maladies, contemporary personal essayists are finally redressing the extreme imbalance that Woolf had noted in her prescient essay. They are, in effect, uniting body and mind in a form that bears witness both to the "astonishing" experience of illness and to the complex nature of self revealed under the pressures of it. In this connection, Mairs's view of her writing seems especially pertinent—"Forced by the exigencies of physical disease to embrace my self in the flesh, I couldn't write bodiless prose. The voice is the creature of the body that produces it. I speak as a crippled woman. . . . No body, no voice; no voice, no body. That's what I know in my bones." Viewed in such a light, the subject of malady seems to offer essayists a rich set of possibilities for the full embodiment of self—body and mind, flesh and spirit. Given such possibilities, essayists who write about their afflictions seem distinctly less interested in the chameleon-like role-playing that has long been a hallmark of the personal essay. These essayists, instead, are more interested in projecting a voice that very closely reflects their own most deeply held sense of themselves, as if there were relatively little distance between their actual and their essayistic selves. Or as Foster puts it, "like the novel and poetry, the personal essay is . . . looking at the cross-purposes of the human psyche, the human heart, yet moving one step closer to experience by its use of the first person singular."

Given the hunger of such essayists to convey "the most intimate and interior dimensions of self," I've been tempted to call their pieces confessional or intimate essays. However, they rarely display the psychological convulsions and heavings up that I associate with confessional poetry. They often create the impression instead of being more self-controlled. Yet they are also energized by an intensity of experience, thought, and feeling that "intimate" does not quite suggest, unless it be "this fucking intimacy" that Harold Brodkey imprecates in his essay on AIDS. So, I'm inclined instead to think of them as "existential" essays, especially because they are so concerned with exploring, expressing, and embodying the self in some of the most pressing circumstances of its existence.

Having lived through such circumstances myself, I can vouch for Woolf's sense of "how astonishing" they can be, "how tremendous the spiritual change," or at least how tremendous the change seems to be when one is in the middle of an extreme affliction or newly recovered from it. Having produced a few pages about my heart attack at the beginning of this piece, I can also affirm Morris's conjecture that "perhaps one of the motives for writing about unspeakable things is the need to pass on a glimpse of something more which comes through living past such experiences." So I've sometimes imagined writing a whole essay about my heart attack. But I don't want to return to all the searing physical and mental experiences I went through back then, especially since I had another attack five years ago on my way home from a cabin in the north woods, so different from the first that now I'd have to do a comparison and contrast—as in, bypasses the first time, stents the second; three weeks hospitalization the first time, four days the second; one week physical therapy the first time, twelve weeks cardiac rehab the second. So much detailed back and forth, it might be more than my heart (or any reader!) could bear.

E|ven now, fifteen years later, I can still see the soap suds in the wine glass, still behold my reflection in the kitchen window that mid-December evening, when out of nowhere, it seemed, I was visited by something like the muse. How else to account for the writing project that suddenly came to mind while doing the dishes? As it first occurred to me that night in the waning days of 1994, the task was relentlessly simple — I would write a brief weather report every day during the coming year, from January first to December thirty-first of 1995. Just a paragraph or two, but enough to produce a detailed record of the year's weather, taking stock of the temperature, wind speed, rainfall, snowfall, and other measurable phenomena, and describing what it looked like and felt like each day on my hillside lot in Iowa City — a place where I'd spent twenty-five years witnessing the flow (and sometimes the clash) of arctic- and gulf-born weather systems. What better to do, I thought, than make something of that experience and the tempestuous weather that often blows my way? What I didn't think of just then is how I could produce a book about the weather without any knowledge of it, except from the perspective of a fanatic vegetable gardener. Nor did it occur to me that anyone might be put off by the prospect of reading incessantly about the weather. For the minute that bizarre project came to mind, it took hold of me like an obsession, so that even Kate, my resident skeptic and wife, came to think I'd go through with it.

Strange as it now seems, the more I thought about the project, the more alluring it became, for it appealed to an intense hunger I was feeling back then to do something completely different from the personal essays and memoirs I'd been reading and teaching and writing about over the previous thirty years. The weather would give me the opportunity to see if I could produce a substantial work of literary nonfiction about something outside of myself, beyond my inner life, something that didn't rely on long-term memory but on a firsthand observation of things that I could put into words like "north wind," "snowfall," "hailstorm," and "hoarfrost"—words that seemed to correspond to the things themselves. The writer's inescapable delusion, but a necessary one, especially for a weather book or any other kind of nature writing. And that's what I fancied myself doing, as if I had the scientific knowledge to be an authentic nature writer.

Given such an irrational presumption, it should come as no surprise that I was also driven by a high and mighty ambition. For by New Year's Day, I thought of my work-to-be as the embodiment of a new literary hybrid—an essayistic journal. Not just a series of brief weather reports as I'd originally planned. But a sustained record of daily observations and reflections, each entry both a free-standing essay in its own right and an episode in the overarching story of the year's weather. A five-hundred-word essay each day, so I wouldn't ever lapse into mere jottings or notations of data. The same average length each day, so that every day and every entry would have equivalent weight in my story of the year's weather. In other words, my work-to-be would ultimately constitute a daybook/essaybook/yearbook all wrapped in one. Or as my best friend called it, "a monstrous personal project." Or, as I told myself in a soothing reverie, "my journal will be something like a Renaissance sonnet sequence, but in this case a contemporary essay sequence, the likes of which has never been tried before." So, it's no wonder that I scoffed at the suggestion of a colleague who advised me early in January not to worry about missing a day now or then. "It's the kind of liberty," he said "that contemporary writers feel free to take now and then." But as I saw it, one could no more skip a day than drop a day from the calendar—or from life itself.

Having settled upon the topic, form, and length of my daily essays, it seemed as if my persona was a foregone conclusion—how else to report things but in a plainly-worded style that would let the weather speak for itself? I would be its friendly, reportorial mouthpiece. A simple enough matter, one might suppose, except that it required me to shed the academic style I'd learned in graduate school and replace it with an unpretentious voice that I found in the no-nonsense guidelines of Strunk and White. In other words, straightforward, declarative sentences in an Anglo-Saxon rather than Latinate vocabulary. And just to be sure that my entries had the ring of a spontaneous diarist, I also decided to enliven my prose with colloquial expressions, sentence fragments, and other conversational usage. How strange it now seems to have made such deliberate decisions about a style that came to feel as if it was second nature. But as with any such change, it required a self-conscious effort to avoid my academic predilections and to develop the style of an observant, straight-talking, spontaneous self. A self that would be suitable for all seasons. With a persona like that, one needn't worry, I thought, about Woolf's cautionary remark in "The Modern Essay"—that "to write daily, to write shortly," one must forsake "the natural richness of the speaking voice." Besides, the weather and its manifold variations would surely endow my prose with the richness of a spoken voice. When New Year's arrived with the first snowfall of winter, it seemed like the heavens had smiled upon my project, especially given the depth and sweep of the snow, which I highlighted in the opening of my first day's essay, like this:

> New Year's Day and a newly fallen snow. Four inches of it, covering the ground with a blanket so vividly white in the morning sun that it makes me wonder why no one ever sings of a white new year. A fresh start. Last year's leavings so well hidden, it's hard for me to believe how green things were just a week ago.

Having launched myself so easily with three sentence fragments and a flurry of one-syllable words, I spent the next few hours taking note of everything I could see, from the rabbit tracks and deer tracks in the early morning snow to the shadows of trees trunks crisscrossing the snow-covered yard at midday. Later that day, I concluded the piece with a report of my impressions during a hike that Kate and I took in mid-afternoon. In other words, I wrote each part shortly after my firsthand observations had taken place, for I wanted the piece to reflect my immediate impressions and reactions—distorted as little as possible by the passage of time and the refraction of memory.

The next few days, the weather turned out to be so striking, so cooperative one might say, that I had plenty to write about—a subzero temperature drop and a corresponding increase at the bird feeders, a midnight snow-walk with Kate, a sudden January thaw. With each set of conditions, the cityscape, the landscape, and the skyscape were variously transformed. And with each set of changes, I adapted the mood of my entries to the weather at hand. Sometimes playful, sometimes solemn, sometimes matter-of-fact—I made my way from day to day, as briskly and changeably as the weather. Glibly taking stock of things even in a dense morning fog:

WEDNESDAY, JANUARY 11
In a great fog, as I discovered this morning, there's no ground at all. No there there. Only here. A fog so dense that even looking out the attic window, I couldn't see any farther than a block away. The familiar background of trees and houses had virtually disappeared, leaving only the foreground of our immediate neighborhood. But that was enough to consume my attention, for yesterday's warm-up to the mid-thirties followed by last night's freezing temperatures had produced a heavy coating of rime on all the shrubs and trees. A patina of hoarfrost backed by a veil of dense fog. White on white. Winter art. A monochromatic landscape.

Rereading that passage now some fifteen years later, I remember how pleasing it was to describe the fog and the rime and the hoarfrost in fragments so crisp as those last four details. The self I had chosen was clearly facile enough—and shallow enough—to get me from day to day without raising any serious questions about the instability and uncertainty inherent in the weather. And with each passing day, I was not only learning how to track the weather and describe it but also how to write about it accurately and evocatively within the five-hundred-word limit that I'd set for myself. Just to make sure that I didn't exceed the limit by more than twenty-five words, I set my word-processing program to produce a page of that approximate length. So whenever the page break appeared, I knew that I had encountered my word limit and would have to pare down what I'd written if I wanted to include additional material. Writing tight, I called it, trimming and trimming again, whenever I had more to say than words to spare. Pacing myself so differently from the leisurely rhythm of a piece like this one that it sometimes seemed as if I was doing a hundred-yard dash rather than a long-distance run. The tempo of one's prose and the tenor of one's voice, I discovered, are subtly but powerfully influenced by the length of one's discourse. In my case, it provoked such an irrepressible impulse to wrap up each entry in one or two pithy sentences that a colleague said I was beginning to sound like a newspaper columnist rather than a journal writer. A telling observation which led me to realize that the elliptical style engendered by my self-imposed word limit was also pushing me toward Baconian epigrams—a mannerism that unconsciously bespeaks a will to dominate things through the power of language.

But it soon became clear that tightening my prose was nothing compared to dealing with the constraints of my topic, especially when the skies were overcast for nine straight days, and those unchanging weather conditions made me wonder what I'd do with the long stretches of hot, sunny, rainless days that usually come in July and August. How would I avoid repetitiousness in midsummer, if I was already having trouble with redundant weather conditions in early winter? To remedy the problem, I decided to expand my horizon a bit and take into account not only our local situation but also conditions around the country and then around the world, given the worldwide influence of the El Niño phenomenon, which was then making its presence felt in Iowa. Actual weather, fictional weather, present, past, and future weather—every aspect of that mysterious phenomenon would be grist for my reports, thanks to a handful of guidebooks and websites that provided me with a treasure-trove of meteorological lore. Given my expanded weather perspective, I also decided to make myself a more expansive and entertaining weatherman, especially after watching a movie version of *Little Women*, so fraught with vivid snow-scenes and other seasonal displays that I devoted a whole entry to its cinematic—and contrived—evocation of the weather. So my reconceived project was well underway, until something happened the evening of January 17 that challenged my complacent role, as I explained the next day:

WEDNESDAY, JANUARY 18
The sky was so clear last night and the moon so bright I could easily see the dark-shaded craters on its surface, when I went out to the compost pile. The air had finally dried out, and the wind died down, leaving a comfortable chill in the high twenties—a perfect winter night for a walk with Pip. But my thoughts were heavily overcast by reports of the catastrophic

earthquake in Japan. Almost two-thousand dead, more than six-thousand injured, and the city of Kobe, a city of almost one and one-half million, burning out of control. In the face of such colossal suffering and loss, my weather-watch suddenly seemed unspeakably trivial and beside the point. And I suddenly felt even more stung by the recollection of Kate's remarks at dinner—"You can't just go on twittering about the sun and the moon. You have to make something more of it." I instinctively wanted to defend myself, to say that I'm not just twittering— that in writing about the sun and the moon and the clouds and the snow, I'm really paying reverence to the things in this world that matter most deeply to me. But the words didn't come readily to my lips, especially when I was savoring the crab-stuffed flounder, steamed artichoke, and chilled sauvignon blanc we were having for dinner. And it wasn't any better this morning, not even during the rare spectacle of watching the sun rise in the east just after I'd seen the full moon set in the west, for I knew that when I went downstairs to get the morning newspaper, the front page would be covered with stories of Kobe. The front page, in fact, offered me a distinctly different kind of sunrise from the one I'd just seen—a full-width color picture, dominated by the reddish-orange sweep of fire raging through the city of Kobe. And above the picture, the haunting remark of Minoru Takasu, a survivor of the quake, just a couple of years older than me—"I thought it was the end of the world."

Again my weather project seemed trivial, especially compared to his remark. But then it occurred to me that I make these reports because, like Minoru Takasu, I cherish the world. I do not want to see the end of it any more than he. I want it to continue, sunrise and sunset, moonrise and moonset, world without end. And I want to take note of its continuance, if for no other reason than to make a record of my reverence for it. Pious sentiments, I realize. But those are the only pieties I know.

In the process of writing that piece, I started to shake and sweat, for I felt more intense about what I was saying there, more emotionally involved, than in any of the preceding entries, thanks to the earthquake, Kate, and Minoru Takasu. Such disturbing provocations that the next day I wrote another essay on Kobe and envisioned myself doing other pieces in that vein, with a more intensely personal slant on things. But two days later, back in the mode of an entertaining weatherman, I did a breezy piece about the north wind, decked out with literary allusions, verbal puns, verse-like echoes, and a snappy conclusion, but strangely aloof from its menacing implications. No wonder one of my graduate students who'd been reading the entries said, "You're keeping people at a distance, allowing them to come this close and no closer."

But I also remember how empowering it felt to produce a carefully wrought, five-hundred-word essay every day—an unprecedented feat, I thought, especially for someone in his sixties. As if age had given me the ability and tenacity to do something I could never have done before. So it seemed all the more urgent to stay in the groove, especially because my daily pieces also made me feel as if I were controlling the weather, as if one could harness such a complex and powerful thing through the magic of language. Talk about an intoxicating venture! I was imbibing it every day, like an addict, from the minute I got up to the moment I went to bed, and often in the middle of the night as well, when I would gaze out the attic windows to check on the moon or the nighttime sky for signs of the next day's weather. How strange that writing, or a misguided conception of it, turned me into a monomaniacal version of myself without realizing it. And only something painfully close to home brought me back to my senses, as I discovered from an experience that took place on Valentine's Day:

TUESDAY, FEBRUARY 14
Thirteen above this morning—a balmy start by comparison
with the last several days. A good omen for St. Valentine's.
But when I put Pip out on his leash, the air must've hit me
the wrong way because it suddenly felt intolerable. So cold, so
harsh, I didn't even want to look at the sky or eyeball the back
yard or anything else outside. I just wanted to get back in as fast
as I could. And when I got back inside, something inside me
almost screamed out what I was feeling just then in every part
of my being. "I've had it. Had it with the cold, the wind, the
ice, the ice-covered driveway, the ice-pack over the backyard,

the iced-over sidewalks, the iced-up car, my ice-nipped ears and toes and fingertips. And the heavy clothing. And the dry air. And the overheated rooms. Everything." Or words to that effect. But Kate was still asleep. I didn't want to wake her up. And besides, the feeling passed so quickly I was left musing upon the suddenness of its appearance as if out of nowhere. Like the dream I'd had just a few hours earlier about the end of the semester. It was the last week of classes, or perhaps exam week, or the week after graduation. No one around. And I was wandering the hallways, looking for someone to talk to, to have coffee with. But all the offices were shut. And no signs of light or life were visible in the gaps between the office doors and the floor. I was standing alone in an empty hallway, in an empty building. Not an uncommon experience when school is out. And sometimes, in fact, a pleasurable image to contemplate, especially in the midst of a semester when the press of students and committees becomes unbearable. But in my dream last night, I felt desolate beyond belief and a great heaving in my chest. An anguish so intense I was suddenly on the verge of tears. And then I awoke, shaking. And then it gradually came to me that I must have been grieving the prospect of my retirement. A strange twist, given the pleasure I've had this semester, on "phased-in retirement," teaching only one course with just a dozen students and a few auditors, who leave me almost completely free to write my daily reports and to contemplate the time when I will be completely free to write, travel, and garden as I wish. I thought I'd adjusted to the chilly side of retirement, just as I thought I'd adjusted to the harshness of winter. But when all is said and done, it must be that I'm troubled by a long run of bitterly cold weather, no matter where it occurs—wide awake or in a dream, in an empty hallway or right outside the back door.

After finishing that piece in mid-morning, I had almost a whole day to mull it over, which enabled me to see that what I had written about there, and perhaps should have been writing about in other entries, was not just the weather outside but the weather inside. Especially given the surprising discovery of my anguish at the prospect of retirement. But the thought of writing about such personal matters day in and day out made me uneasy, for it seemed like a self-regarding activity that I didn't want to indulge just because of a bad dream, though two years later, in February 1997, I started such a journal when the bad dream suddenly turned into a waking nightmare three months before my impending retirement. In February 1995, though, I was still committed to producing emotionally restrained pieces about tangible things in the world of my daily experience—pieces in the spirit of E. B. White, my onetime literary idol, whose personal essays are so carefully buttoned-down that more often than not they only hint at the depth of his emotions. Yet White would never have been content with so confining a subject as the weather. Even during World War II, when he withdrew to his saltwater farm in Maine, he wrote not only about life on his farm and in the nearby town of Brooklin, but also about events taking place around the country and the world. So it seemed reasonable to shift my primary focus from the weather to my vegetable garden as well as the entire world of my daily experience, including Kate, our dog Pip, our cat Phoebe, as well as the gardens, trees, and shrubs on our three-quarter-acre lot. Also the wild animals that lived on our land or that passed through it. Groundhogs, moles, possums, rabbits, deer, raccoons, and squirrels—all the vermin that trouble the heart of an ardent vegetable gardener. Also our neighbors, our neighborhood, the university where I taught, as well as other places and people I encountered or thought about on my walks in the city of Iowa City where I live. In other words, I would write about virtually everything in my life, but without dwelling on the internal weather of my life—or at least not so overtly or extensively as to become too personal. I'd be personal without being personal.

What I didn't realize was that in opening the journal to the full scope of my life, I would inevitably be compelled to write about the inner storms as well as the outer ones. It was only a few weeks, in fact, before my feelings were engaged, when Phoebe, our twenty-year-old cat, came up with a cancerous tumor, and I was deeply anguished over the prospect of her demise. Then a few weeks later, an unpleasant episode at the university drew the full force of my anger, and shortly after that, in mid-May, the recurrence of Kate's breast cancer drew the full force of my panic. So, as May gave way to June, I felt compelled to track the diagnosis of her condition as closely as I had been observing the weather, my vegetable garden, the university, and Phoebe. Especially given the fact that one doctor considered Kate's tumor to be merely a local recurrence at the point of the previous surgery, whereas another specialist, whom my brother referred to as "the doctor from hell," considered it to be the mark of a systemic, and therefore incurable, condition. Torn between two such radically different views of her condition and her fate, my essays of that period were as emotionally varied and unstable as spring weather. By early June, I'd become so preoccupied with the uncertainty and instability all around me — including my neighbor Jim's attempt to identify the sex of a groundhog which was then threatening my garden — that I ended one of my pieces with the following reflection:

> The more I've thought about it, everything seems to be on the move — from the sex of the groundhog to the status of El Niño to the diagnosis of Kate. As if everything were playing possum. Dead one minute, alive the next. Female one day, male the next. So, I'm beginning to feel uncertain about everything. I mean, if I can't trust my own eyes, or Jim's animal know-how, or the weather service's prediction, or a doctor's opinion, what can I rely on? My colleagues worry about problematic literary texts. But right now the whole world looks problematic to me.

Two days later, still vexed by the problematic nature of things, I wrote the following piece, so completely interiorized, so given over to self-flagellation that it seems like the work of a completely different person from the self-confident one who just a few months before had been writing dispassionate weather reports:

SATURDAY, JUNE 10
My son, Marshall, called this morning, and I'd just finished telling him about the disagreement between Kate's cancer surgeon and the Doctor from Hell, when Marshall said, "It must be really difficult to be faced with two such different interpretations." Initially, it *was* difficult to understand how one doctor could treat her recent cancer as just a local recurrence while the other believed it to be systemic. Far worse was the

hopeless future that seemed in store for Kate, according to the Doctor from Hell, who repeatedly asserted that her cancer was systemic and therefore certain to recur. "Maybe, it won't come back for four or five years. Or it could suddenly show up everywhere in the system six months from now." But once my brother explained how unlikely it would be for a cell to travel throughout Kate's entire system and return exactly to the site of her last breast cancer, I've not had any trouble weighing the merits of the doctors' radically different interpretations. Now, instead, I'm troubled by how quickly I was willing to accept the extreme diagnosis of the Doctor from Hell. Oh yes, I was initially puzzled, so I asked him how all the tests could be negative, yet the cancer be systemic. But once he began talking about the crudity of the tests and then told me to think about a dandelion gone to seed and the difficulty of finding its seed in the grass, my skepticism was readily dispelled.

As I look back on that afternoon, I wonder why I was so quick to accept the opinion of someone I'd never met before, even though it contradicted the view of the distinguished cancer surgeon who's been taking excellent care of Kate for the past six and a half years. Partly, I think it was the unusual frankness with which the Doctor from Hell announced his dire view of things. Partly his highly articulate manner, so different from the uncomfortable behavior of the surgeon, who usually says little and explains much less. But ultimately, I think the dandelion metaphor took me in, for it spoke to me in terms I know from firsthand observation. Kate, as usual took a more hard-nosed view of things. "Didn't you notice how I was trying to lead him on, to see how far he'd go. I've always known that it can recur, but the way he was talking just didn't make sense to me, not in terms of the evidence from the tests. And besides, he didn't have any research studies to back up what he was saying. Even he admitted that."

So, I can't help wondering why I too didn't notice the weakness of his case. I've been chiding students for years whenever they don't provide evidence for their assertions. And why didn't I tell him that his dandelion analogy was badly chosen, for the body is not like a lawn any more than a cancer cell is like a dandelion seed. Maybe, it's because the dandelion analogy did embody a germ of common sense — that some things are so small they cannot be detected even by the most sophisticated technology. But a germ of sense doesn't necessarily lead to an epidemic of truth.

Looking back on those reflections, I'm fascinated to see how much my voice had changed — altered, it would seem, as a result of being distressed by Kate's situation, by the differing diagnoses of her condition, and by my failure to assess them with a properly critical eye. In other words, my voice had changed under the press of circumstances, rather than the force of a consciously willed choice such as I had made to begin with. And I didn't immediately notice the difference, partly because I was so distressed, but also because I mistakenly thought that I was still writing in the plain and simple style of my early weather reports, whereas my diction in that entry had become more polysyllabic and my syntax more complex, more intricately balanced, more rhetorically heightened. How strange, to think of my persona as having changed without being aware of it, as if I'd undergone a drastic facial transformation without taking note of it in the mirror. How often, I wonder, do we hear ourselves on paper? How often do we listen to the changes taking place in our voice; how often do we take stock of our morphing selves? Montaigne listened to himself incessantly, and the more he listened the more voices he heard. But my ear was so attuned to the changes all around me that by contrast I came to feel almost Gibraltar-like in my stability. For whatever strange turns the world might take, and whatever might happen to Phoebe and Kate, I arose each morning devoted to producing a five-hundred-word essay, and each day without fail I completed a piece before going to bed. Pieces about everything from the progress of my tomatoes to the breakdown of our air-conditioner on the hottest night of the summer. So, in a sense, my daily essays enabled me to transcend the vicissitudes of the weather, of experience, and all that flesh is heir to.

Yet my voice was not only changing, but the changes were taking place more often than I might have imagined, for just a couple of weeks after the stylistic complexities of that interiorized piece about the differing diagnoses, I was back in something like my earlier voice, almost as plain in style as before, in this entry about our Welsh terrier, Pip.

Kate and I were kneeling on the ground, looking at Pip, his eyes glazed, his body limp. We were trying to figure out what had caused him to vomit and then go into something like shock, when just a few minutes before he'd been prancing around a tree while Kate worked in her flower bed. So I went to get our neighbor Jim, who knows more about animals than anyone around, but after a few minutes without much improvement, we all agreed that a trip to the vet was in order. And it was. Pip had evidently eaten something that caused him so much pain and panic he'd almost gone into a severe shock. So today, tomorrow, and Monday, he's on stomach relaxants, fluids, and light food. And he's been acting the part whenever he sees me. Head down, tail between his legs, moping over the absence of his usual rations and treats, especially the rawhide chips that probably caused some of the trouble.

But the real trouble that's got me feeling a bit hangdog too is that Pip's clearly aging, as Kate's been trying to tell me whenever we have an episode like this. "I keep telling you I've been running a geriatric ward around here the past year." But I guess I've been ignoring her, because Pip has generally had such a good constitution, so few illnesses, such a handsome, well-marked coat—full black saddle, reddish brown legs and head—that he often seems to be just a few years old. And often he still behaves that way, wanting to get ahead of us on a walk, even when he doesn't have any idea of where we're going, sometimes taking the leash in his mouth and jumping around with it, like a young puppy. But he's ten years old—old for his breed, according to the vet. His eyes are beginning to cloud up a bit, his stomach is evidently beginning to act up a bit, he doesn't wake up early anymore, and he doesn't try to run away much anymore, as he did just a year or two ago. It used to be that instead of calling Jim to diagnose an ailment, I'd be imploring him to help me track Pip down, usually at ten or eleven in the evening. Probably that's why Jim was so surprised by his behavior last night.

But I don't mean to be writing an obituary here. I'm just taking stock of things, noting the seasonal changes. Besides, Jim's help last night gave me a good excuse to give him and

Carol one of the five heads of cauliflower I harvested this morning. One good head deserves another. And it was especially good at lunch today, when Kate served one steamed and cooled, dressed with a Creole vinaigrette.

I can still remember making that entry, for the words came so readily to mind that it seemed as if I was transcribing them rather than composing them, taking dictation rather than writing a piece of literary nonfiction. The ultimate payoff, I thought, for the straightforward style I'd been honing the previous six months. What I didn't realize just then was that the words came quickly not just because I was in a stylistic groove and the groove of a five-hundred-word essay, but because I was in possession of an outlook, a way of thinking about things—an intense consciousness of time, change, and mortality—that had begun to take shape with the discovery of Phoebe's tumor and the recurrence of Kate's breast cancer, and that colored many of my pieces the rest of that year, particularly given an exceptionally severe mid-summer drought and heat-wave that ravaged crops, livestock, and people throughout the Midwest. Thus in looking now at that entry about Pip, I'm struck not only by its prose style but also by its air of sadness, by its retrospective turn of mind, as if the persona inhabiting the piece were quite a bit older and more hangdog than the self-assured fellow who was making weather reports six months back. Same style but drastically different voices—so different they ultimately led me to question my longtime supposition that style is the overriding determinant of voice. In the backward abysm of time, that supposition so beguiled me that I created a course called "Style and Voice," in which I required students to write up the same memory in four or five distinctly different styles. A sequence of assignments intended to show how different stylistic choices inevitably alter both the depiction of an experience and the projection of one's self. But I've come to believe in recent years that the self inhabiting a piece of prose is the product of so many things in addition to style—the length of a piece, as well as its form, its mode, its mood, its gist, its pacing, its point of view, its state of mind—that "gestalt" is the only word I can think of to suggest the multiplicity and complexity of its determinants. Change any one of them, and you alter most of the others—and by extension the whole gestalt.

Why so long, one might ask, to arrive at such a self-evident truth—as if it were news that the whole is greater than the sum of its parts? I'm tempted to answer that question by taking refuge in the obvious—in the memory of my former attachment to a notion of voice so closely linked to the sound of the words, to the structure and rhythm of a sentence, that it seemed to be engendered more by style than by anything else. And why such a fierce attachment to so reductive an idea? What else, but the inescapable hunger for control—in one's thinking, one's teaching, and one's writing. Control the words and you control everything—a comfortable and convenient idea, especially for a teacher of writing. But how to account for those moments when the words come quickly as if from nowhere, in a rush that seems like nothing so much as the welling up of things from deep within? Such moments, of course, are neither teachable nor explicable, but their occurrence is indisputable. By late August, for example, when Phoebe was gone and the walnut leaves began to yellow and fall, I was having so many such moments that my journal often seemed to be writing itself. And not just in elegiac essays but also in zestful and hedonistic pieces. In the face of mortality, what else to do but seize the day? All of which led me to feel that I finally had a glimmering of what people mean when they speak of finding one's voice—an expression that had often troubled me before, because it suggested a mystical and static idea of self. And yet for the rest of that journal, I had found a voice and found it not just in a style but in a state of mind—in an awareness and acceptance of time and change that moved me to write about my daily experience without the self-conscious deliberation of my earlier entries. So, I came to think of that journal as having saved my life, and not just because it helped me through a difficult time in my life, or because I turned it into two published daybooks about my life, *Weathering Winter* and *My Vegetable Love*, but because it led me to see how a voice can give rise to life, invoke life, embody life, particularly when it is animated by one's deepest convictions.

That said, I should also acknowledge that the day after I stopped keeping the journal, I felt a great sense of relief at not having to write anything that day, though I made a brief entry just in case I might need something for a postscript. And the day after that another brief entry, as well as a great sense of exhaustion and bone-racking pain—a message from my body, according to Kate, of the stress I'd been putting on myself (and her). And the next five days another batch of shorter and shorter entries, evidently the sign of an inner momentum running down, an inner need pouring itself out. And then at last the feeling that I had finally put that voice to rest — only to discover a year or so later during the angst of impending retirement that it was still seemingly there, suddenly roused to vent itself in another book-length journal, followed by a promise to Kate that I would never undertake another such project — a promise I kept until she was suddenly swept away by a cerebral hemorrhage. And then my voice returned yet again, having its say once again in a year of letters to Kate. A life after death in language. So, I've sometimes been tempted to think that the voice I found when Kate was still alive is a voice for all seasons. Still with me, though she's long gone. And yet when I recently gave a reading from *Letters to Kate*, I heard such a different person from the days of that gardening journal fifteen years ago — a person so burdened by loss and grief — that I wonder how I could possibly have thought they were akin. Especially given the difference between journal entries and love letters. How often do we listen to ourselves on paper? How often do we hear our morphing selves? How often do we heed the weather reports? Change, after all, is in the air — it touches us, touches our words, touches our personae, as it touches all things. So, a voice for all seasons could only exist in a world without change, a life without death. The "I" is mutable, whether we will it or not.

ACKNOWLEDGMENTS

This book is the outgrowth of courses in prose style, voice, and the art of the personal essay that I began teaching at the University of Iowa during the 1960s, well before the academic advent of literary nonfiction, thanks to the encouragement and professional support of such a visionary department chair as John C. Gerber and my colleague, Richard Lloyd-Jones. To both of them, I'm especially grateful for guiding me toward this work. I'm also very grateful to my friend Robert Scholes, whose invitation during the late 1960s to collaborate on a little textbook, *Elements of the Essay*, gave me the first opportunity to put in print some of my thoughts about the chameleon-like person in the personal essay. Likewise, I'm grateful to Chris Anderson, whose invitation during the mid 1980s to do a piece about essayists on the essay led me toward research that was fundamental to the central idea of this book. And I'm grateful to David Hamilton for his keen editorial reactions to some of my early pieces on the essay that he published during the 1990s in the *Iowa Review*.

My work on this book was generously supported by research leaves and grants for which I am very grateful to the University of Iowa. Colleagues and students have also helped me in numerous ways. For assistance in discovering and discussing essayistic commentary on the essay, I'm particularly grateful to Ned Stuckey-French and other members of the "Essay Reading Group," Maura Brady, Cassie Kircher, Michele Payne, John Price, and Dan Roche. For assistance in discovering British and Burmese manuals pertaining to hangings, I'm very grateful to my colleague Miriam Gilbert. For their thoughtful reactions to draft versions or early versions of essays in this book, I'm grateful to Marilyn Abildskov, Trudy Dittmar, Hope Edelman, Rebecca Faery, Janis Forman, Patricia Foster, Eugene Garber, Laura Julier, Michele Morano, Jeff Porter, and Kathleen Blake Yancey. For their generosity in reading and responding to the entire manuscript, I'm very grateful to Janet Burroway,

Carol de Saint Victor, John Kulka, Robert Scholes, David Shields, and Garrett Stewart.

The University of Iowa Press, as always, has been a publisher par excellence, thanks to Joe Parsons, who read the manuscript during a busy time in his schedule and gave me a very encouraging response, as well as to Holly Carver, whose editorial oversight, detailed suggestions, thoughtful reactions, and enthusiastic support are beyond compare.

WORKS CITED

Addison, Joseph, and Richard Steele. Spectator, No. 476. *Selected Essays from the Tatler and the Spectator*, ed. Warren L. Fleischauer. Los Angeles: Gateway Editions, 1956. 164–65.

Adorno, T. W. "The Essay as Form," trans. Bob Hullot-Kentor. *New German Critique* 31 (Spring-Summer 1984): 151–71.

Allen, Woody. "Random Reflections of a Second-Rate Mind." *The Best American Essays 1991*, ed. Joyce Carol Oates and Robert Atwan. New York: Ticknor and Fields, 1991. 1–8.

Anonymous [Virginia Woolf]. "Modern Essays." *Times Literary Supplement*, 30 November 1922: 1–2.

Bacon, Francis. *The Advancement of Learning.* Oxford: Oxford English Texts, 1974.

Baldwin, James. *The Price of the Ticket: Collected Nonfiction, 1948–1985.* New York, St. Martins, 1985.

Beerbohm, Max. *And Even Now.* London: William Heinemann, 1920.

———. *Letters of Max Beerbohm, 1892–1956*, ed. Rupert Hart-Davis. London: Murray, 1988.

———. *Yet Again.* London: William Heinemann, 1928.

Benson, Arthur. "The Art of the Essayist." http://essays.quotidiana.org/benson/art_of_the_essayist/

Brodkey, Harold. *This Wild Darkness: The Story of My Death.* New York: Holt, 1997.

Broyard, Anatole. *Intoxicated by My Illness: And Other Writings on Life and Death.* New York: Ballantine, 1993.

Cofer, Judith Ortiz. *The Latin Deli: Prose and Poetry.* Athens: University of Georgia Press, 1993.

D'Agata, John. *Halls of Fame.* St. Paul: Graywolf, 2001.

———. "1500 B.C.E." *The Lost Origins of the Essay.* St. Paul: Graywolf, 2009. 9.

Daiches, David. "Reflections on the Essay." *A Century of the Essay.* New York: Harcourt, 1951. 1–8.

Didion, Joan. "On Keeping a Notebook." *Slouching Towards Bethlehem.* New York: Farrar, Straus and Giroux, 2008. 84–130.

————. *The White Album.* New York: Farrar, Straus and Giroux, 1990.

Dillard, Annie. *Teaching a Stone to Talk: Expeditions and Encounters.* New York: Simon and Schuster, 1982.

Dittmar, Trudy. *Fauna and Flora, Earth and Sky: Brushes with Nature's Wisdom.* Iowa City: University of Iowa Press, 2003.

Early, Gerald. "Life with Daughters: Watching the Miss America Pageant." *Kenyon Review* (Autumn 1990): 132–45.

————. Introduction. *Tuxedo Junction: Essays on American Culture.* New York: Ecco Press, 1989. vii–xvii.

Eiseley, Loren. *The Immense Journey.* New York: Random House, 1957.

Elbow, Peter. *Writing with Power.* New York: Oxford University Press, 1981.

Elkin, Stanley. *Pieces of Soap.* New York: Simon and Schuster, 1992.

Ephron, Nora. "Revision and Life." *Nora Ephron Collected.* Avon: New York, 1991. 213–16.

Fitzgerald, F. Scott. "The Crackup." *Esquire,* February 1936.

Foster, Patricia, ed. *Minding the Body: Women Writers on Body and Soul.* New York: Anchor: 1994.

Foster, Patricia, and Mary Swander, ed. *The Healing Circle: Authors Writing of Recovery.* New York: Plume, 1998.

Gass, William. "Emerson and the Essay." *Habitations of the Word.* New York: Simon and Schuster, 1985. 9–49.

Gerould, Katherine Fullerton. "An Essay on Essays." *North American Review* 240:3 (December 1935): 409–18.

Gornick, Vivian. "On the Street." *Approaching Eye Level.* Boston: Beacon Press, 1996. 1–29.

————. *The Situation and the Story: The Art of Personal Narrative.* New York: Farrar, Straus and Giroux, 2001.

Graham, Paul. "The River." http://www.paulgraham.com/essay.html.

Grealy, Lucy. *Autobiography of a Face.* New York: Harper, 2003.

Griffin, Susan. *Eros of Everyday Life.* New York: Doubleday, 1995.

Halsbury's Statutes of England. Vol. 5. London: Butterworth, 1948.

Hardwick, Elizabeth. Introduction. *The Best American Essays, 1986,* ed. Elizabeth Hardwick and Robert Atwan. New York: Ticknor and Fields, 1986. xiii–xxi.

Hazlitt, William. *The Complete Works of William Hazlitt.* London: Dent, 1931.

Hoagland, Edward. *The Tugman's Passage.* New York: Random House, 1982.

Hooper, Judith. "Beauty Tips for the Dead." *Minding the Body: Women Writers on Body and Soul*, ed. Patricia Foster. New York: Anchor, 1994. 107–38.

Huxley, Aldous. Preface. *Collected Essays*. New York: Harper, 1960. v–ix.

Kakutani, Michiko. "Joan Didion: Staking Out California." *New York Times Magazine*, 10 June 1979.

Kazin, Alfred. "The Essay as a Modern Form." *The Open Form: Essays for Our Time*, ed. Alfred Kazin. New York: Harcourt, 1961. vii–xi.

Klaus, Carl H. "Essayists on the Essay." *Literary Nonfiction: Theory, Criticism, and Pedagogy*, ed. Chris Anderson. Carbondale: Southern Illinois University Press, 1989. 155–75.

———. *Letters to Kate: Life After Life*. Iowa City: University of Iowa Press, 2006.

———. *My Vegetable Love: A Journal of a Growing Season*. Boston: Houghton Mifflin, 1996.

———. *Taking Retirement: A Beginner's Diary*. Boston: Beacon Press, 1999.

———. *Weathering Winter: A Gardener's Daybook*. Iowa City: University of Iowa Press, 1997.

Krutch, Joseph Wood. "No Essays, Please." *Saturday Review of Literature*, 10 March 1951: 18–19, 35.

Lamb, Charles. *The Complete Works*. New York: Modern Library, 1935.

———. *Essays of Elia*. Iowa City: University of Iowa Press, 2003.

———. Unpublished Review of Hazlitt's *Table Talk*. *Lamb as Critic*, ed. Roy Park. Lincoln: University of Nebraska Press, 1980. 299–307.

———. *Letters of Charles and Mary Lamb*, ed. E. V. Lucas. London: Methuen and Company, 1904.

London Magazine, 1820–1825. http://onlinebooks.library.upenn.edu/webbin/serial?id=londonmag.

Lopate, Phillip. *Against Joie de Vivre*. New York: Poseidon Press, 1989.

———. *The Art of the Personal Essay: An Anthology from the Classical Era to the Present*. New York: Anchor, 1994.

———. "The Essay Lives—In Disguise." *New York Times Book Review*, 18 November 1984: 1, 47–49.

———. Foreword. *Essays of Elia*, by Charles Lamb. Iowa City: University of Iowa Press, 2003. vii–xx.

Mairs, Nancy. *Carnal Acts*. New York: HarperCollins, 1990.

———. *Plaintext*. New York: HarperCollins, 1986.

———. *Voice Lessons: On Becoming a Woman Writer*. Boston: Beacon Press, 1994.

Malcolm, Janet. "41 False Starts." The *New Yorker*, 11 July 1994.

Manual of Rules for the Superintendence and Management of Jails in Burma. Rangoon: Government Printing, 1920.

McPhee, John. "The Search for Marvin Gardens." *Pieces of the Frame*. New York: Farrar, Straus and Giroux, 1975. 75–92.

Monson, Ander. "Essay as Hack." http://otherelectricities.com/swarm/ essayashack.html.

Montaigne, Michel de. *The Complete Essays of Montaigne*, trans. Donald M. Frame. Stanford: Stanford University Press, 1957.

Morris, Adalaide. "Cuttings." *Sonora Review* 20 (Winter 1991): 10–20.

Nelson, Maggie. *Bluets*. Seattle: Wave Books, 2009.

Oates, Joyce Carol. "My Father, My Fiction." *New York Times Book Review*, 19 March 1989.

———. *(Woman) Writer: Occasions and Opportunities*. New York: Dutton, 1988.

Orwell, George. *The Collected Essays, Letters, and Journalism of George Orwell*, ed. Sonia Orwell and Ian Angus. New York: Harcourt Brace, 1968.

Ozick, Cynthia. "She: Portrait of the Essay as a Warm Body." *Quarrel and Quandry*. New York: Vintage, 2001.

Report of the Royal Commission on Capital Punishment 1949–1953. London: Her Majesty's Stationery Office, September 1953.

Repplier, Agnes. "The Essay in Wartime." *Yale Review* (January 1918): 249–59.

Rhys, Ernest, ed. *Modern English Essays*. London: J. M. Dent, 1922.

Rodriguez, Richard. *Hunger of Memory: The Education of Richard Rodriguez*. New York: David Godine, 1982.

Sanders, Scott Russell. "The Singular First Person." *Essayists on the Essay: Redefining the Genre*, ed. Alexander Butrym. Athens: University of Georgia Press, 1989. 31–42.

Scholes, Robert, and Carl H. Klaus. *Elements of the Essay*. New York: Oxford University Press, 1969.

Shields, David. *Reality Hunger: A Manifesto*. New York: Alfred Knopf, 2010.

Silko, Leslie Marmon. *Yellow Woman and a Beauty of Spirit*. New York: Touchstone Books, 1997.

Strunk, William, and E. B. White. *The Elements of Style*. New York: Harper and Row, 1959.

Stephen, Leslie. "The Essayists." *Men, Books, and Manners.*
Minneapolis: University of Minnesota Press, 1956. 45–73.

Trow, George. *The Harvard Black Rock Forest.* Iowa City: University of
Iowa Press, 2004.

Walker, Alice. *In Search of Our Mothers' Gardens.* San Diego: Harcourt
Brace, 1983.

Wallace, David Foster. *A Supposedly Fun Thing I'll Never Do Again.*
Boston: Little Brown, 1997.

Weathers, Winston. *An Alternate Style: Options in Composition.*
Portsmouth: Boynton/Cook, 1980.

White, E. B. "Dear Mr. 0214 1063 02 10730 08." *New York Times,*
23 September 1987.

———. Draft Versions of "Dear Mr. 0214 1063 02 10730 08."
E. B. White Collection, Cornell University Library.

———. *Essays of E. B. White.* New York: Harper, 1977.

———. *One Man's Meat.* New York: Harper, 1944.

———. *Letters of E. B. White,* ed. Dorothy Lobrano Guth and Martha
White. New York: HarperCollins, 2006.

Willcox, Louise Collier. "Some Recent Essays." *North American Review*
(1906): 780–91.

Williams, William Carlos. *Imaginations.* New York: New Directions,
1970.

Winer, Joyce. "The Floating Lightbulb." *Minding the Body: Women
Writers on Body and Soul,* ed. Patricia Foster. New York: Anchor:
1994. 33–52.

Wolfe, Tom. *The Kandy-Kolored Tangerine-Flake Streamline Baby.* New
York: Farrar, Straus and Giroux, 1965.

Wolff, Geoffrey. "Introduction: An Apprentice." *Best American Essays
1989,* ed. Geoffrey Wolff and Robert Atwan. New York: Ticknor &
Fields, 1989. 13–35.

———, ed. *The New Journalism.* New York: Harper and Row, 1973.

Woolf, Virginia. *The Common Reader.* Harcourt Brace, 1953.

———. *The Essays of Virginia Woolf,* Volume One, 1904–1912, ed.
Andrew McNellie. San Diego: Harcourt Brace, 1986.

———. *The Essays of Virginia Woolf,* Volume Two, 1912–1918, ed.
Andrew McNellie. San Diego: Harcourt Brace, 1987.

———. *The Essays of Virginia Woolf,* Volume Three, 1919–1924, ed.
Andrew McNellie. San Diego: Harcourt Brace, 1988.

———. *The Essays of Virginia Woolf,* Volume Four, 1925–1928, ed.
Andrew McNellie. San Diego: Harcourt Brace, 2008.

————. *The Essays of Virginia Woolf*, Volume Five, 1929–1932, ed. Stuart N. Clarke. San Diego: Harcourt Brace, 2009.

————. *Night and Day*. San Diego: Harcourt, 1973.

Wright, Richard. *Uncle Tom's Children*. New York: Library of America, 1991.

INDEX

Fitzgerald, F. Scott, 120
Foster, Patricia, 126–127

Gass, William, 12, 19, 22; "Emerson and the Essay," 19, 22
Gerould, Katherine Fullerton, 12, 19
Gornick, Vivian, 1, 39; "On the Street," 34; *The Situation and the Story*, 2
Graham, Paul, 21
Grealy, Lucy, 121
Griffin, Susan: "Red Shoes," 34

Hardwick, Elizabeth, 12, 19
Hazlitt, William, 45, 58, 66, 75; "On Familiar Style," 45
Hoagland, Edward, 12, 19, 46, 47, 48, 58, 74; "What I Think, What I Am," 2, 39
Hooper, Judith, 121
Hunt, Leigh, 70
Huxley, Aldous, 21

Johnson, Samuel, 66

Kazin, Alfred, 12, 19, 20, 21
Klaus, Carl H.: essayistic journal, 133–147; *Letters to Kate*, 147; *My Vegetable Love*, 146; *Weathering Winter*, 146

Lamb, Charles, 1, 45, 58, 60–73, 79, 89, 96; accused by Southey, 68; "A Bachelor's Complaint against Married Couples," 96; "A Character of the Late Elia," 64; "A Chapter on Ears," 70, 71; "Christ's Hospital Five and Thirty Years Ago," 69; "The Convalescent," 67; "A Dissertation upon Roast Pig," 60–61, 71–73; "Dream Children," 71; "Elia," 60–73; *Elia: Essays Published under That Signature in the London Magazine*, 65; friendship with Samuel Taylor Coleridge, 69; "Grace before Meat," 71; letter to Barron Field, 63; letter to Charles Ollier, 65; letter to John Taylor, 63; letter to Samuel Taylor Coleridge, 72; "Mackery End in Hertfordshire," 67; "Modern Gallantry," 68, 69, 71; "My Relations," 67; "New Year's Eve," 67; "Old Benchers of the Inner Temple," 67; "Oxford in the Vacation," 64, 69, 71; as published in *London Magazine*, 61, 65; "Recollections of Christ's Hospital," 65, 69; renaming of brother and sister, 67; response to Leigh Hunt's review, 70; review of William Hazlitt's *Table Talk*, 1, 66; "The South Sea House," 61–64, 66, 67, 68, 71
Lawrence, D. H., 49
Little Women, 136
Lopate, Phillip, 2, 21, 58, 74, 96; "Against Joie de Vivre," 96; foreword to *The Essays of Elia*, 2; "The Essay Lives — In Disguise," 19
Lynd, Robert, 76–77, 79

Mairs, Nancy, 2, 47, 48, 58, 74, 120, 121, 122, 123, 124–125, 126, 130; "But First," 2; *Car-*

49–59, 74, 89, 124; "Bedfellows," 124; "Dear Mr. 0214 1063 02 10730 08," 50–52; "The Geese," 41, 52–57, 59; letter to Margo Todd, 2; letter to Scott Elledge, 124; "Once More to the Lake," 30, 52–57, 59, 91; *One Man's Meat*, 3, 30; "The Ring of Time," 41, 52–57, 59; "Spring," 30–31, 32, 35, 37, 40; "The Summer Catarrh," 124

Williams, William Carlos: "An Essay on Virginia," 39

Willcox, Louise Collier, 127

Winer, Joyce, 121, 122–123

Wolfe, Tom: "Kandy-Kolored Tangerine-Flake Streamline Baby," 31; *The New Journalism*, 32

Wolff, Geoffrey, 48

Woolf, Virginia, 1, 2, 39, 45, 46, 73, 74–85, 123, 129–130, 131; *The Common Reader*, 74, 82; "The Decay of Essay Writing," 75–76; and her father, 75; "A Flying Lesson," 78; on Hazlitt, 85, 89; "Impressions of Leslie Stephen," 78; "The Modern Essay," 2, 45, 74, 79, 134; "Modern Essays," 74, 78, 79, 85; *Night and Day*, 78; "On Being Ill," 85, 123, 129; review of Robert Lynd's essays, 76–77

Wright, Richard: "The Ethics of Living Jim Crow," 89